TOPGUN ZEN

The Importance of Mysticism, Science, Air Combat and Daily Life

by
Barry Kaigen McMahon

Llumina Press

© 2009 Barry Kaigen McMahon

All rights reserved. No part of this publication may be reproduced or transmitted in any form or by any means electronic or mechanical, including photocopy, recording, or any information storage and retrieval system, without permission in writing from both the copyright owner and the publisher.

Requests for permission to make copies of any part of this work should be mailed to Permissions Department, Llumina Press, 6341 NW 61st Ave Ocala, FL 34482.

ISBN: 978-1-62550-431-9 (PB)
    978-1-60594-369-5 (HC)
    978-1-60594-370-1 (Ebook)

For my teachers Koryu Roshi, Maezumi Roshi and Tenshin Roshi…without whom I would have no understanding.

For my family, Robert, Pauline, Jason, Bobby, Kim, Dana, Tyson, Kathie, Chris, Ayden, Sorenne, Ava and Kyle….without whom I would have no love.

And for my wife, Nicolee…without whom I would have no joy.

Man has two eyes

One only sees what moves in fleeting time

The other

What is eternal and divine

                                        The Book of Angelus Silesius

TABLE OF CONTENTS

Acknowledgments   i
Introduction   iii

PART ONE
THE ABSOLUTE

Chapter One
Topgun Zen…The Importance of the Journey   1

Chapter Two
The Teaching of Emptiness…The Importance of Mu   12

Chapter Three
The Price of Apples…The Importance of Physics   27

Chapter Four
The Absolute Light…The Importance of Einstein   39

Chapter Five
No Such Thing as a Small Thing…The Importance of Quantum Mechanics ….   57

PART TWO
THE RELATIVE

Chapter Six
Desire's Clear Light…The Importance of Suffering   85

Chapter Seven

The Devil's Advocate...The Importance of Natural Instinct and Well-Being...   108

Chapter Eight

A Tale of Well-Being...The Importance of Mutiny on the Bounty   127

Chapter Nine

Sword-fighting and Air Combat...The Importance of Zen in Action   150

Chapter Ten

The Delusion of Appearances...The Importance of Compassion In the Realm of Violence   164

Conclusion   187

ACKNOWLEDGEMENTS

First I'd like to thank my parents, Robert and Pauline McMahon, whose love and determination to raise their boys in a stable home and provide us with the best education possible was the foundation for our lives that have been well lived.

Secondly, deep bows for my main teachers in the dharma, Osaka Koryru Roshi, Taizan Maezumi Roshi and Charles Tenshin Fletcher Roshi, whose teachings and guidance has been invaluable in my life and development.

For my appreciation of physics, I have to mainly thank Professors Richard Wolfson and Brian Greene, whose works have made the often obscure world of modern physics accessible to the layman. In this regard, I would also like to extend my thanks to Prof. Daniel Sheehan of the University of San Diego who clarified certain difficult aspects of modern physics for me.

I want to thank those who were kind enough to read my manuscript and provide valuable suggestions: Tyson Miller, Ken Deeble, Steve Gelb, Maryrita Hillengas, Charles Tenshin Fletcher Roshi and Dave Dohi Scott Sensei, and also David Paul for the wonderful cover design. Their encouragement and ideas were instrumental is seeing the book through to its conclusion.

And finally, I'd like to thank my loving wife, Nicolee McMahon Roshi, not only for the deep debt I owe her for her teachings and example in the dharma, but also for countless hours of editing and honest criticism.

INTRODUCTION

Zen is important because it has the power to liberate us from the neurologically inherited and culturally conditioned delusions of the human mind. It's that simple. And it's that difficult.

The most basic inherited delusion is the feeling, the sense, the idea and even the belief that I am...alone. This sense of self as ultimately separate from the rest of existence is something all humans can attest to, yet has been addressed by Buddhism for millennia as the root cause of our suffering. But Buddhism in general, and certainly Zen in particular, claims that the essence of enlightenment is the realization that, as Shakyamuni Buddha exclaimed upon his own realization, "I alone...AM!" When the Ghordian knot of delusion is cut, the lonely and anguished precipice of self disintegrates in the light of a new understanding.

But when we are born in this world, and trained to function within it with delusions accepted as fact, we cannot avoid suffering. As we have said, the first and most basic of these is that I exist (as a separate being). The second is that, I know what reality is. A third follows naturally from the first two; namely, that I know what is real, and those that don't agree with me must be wrong.

The first of these problems, simply, the existence of the self, sets up a dualistic world view which leads to endless conflict with what is not I, and by extension, not mine. The Western philosophic tradition, both before and after Descartes, would find the existence of the self an inescapable tenet of honest perception, but to Zen, this is without a doubt not only a delusion, but also a huge cause of individual and collective suffering.

The second problem, I know what reality is, and third, those who don't agree with me must be wrong, follow naturally from the first. Since I am, and I perceive the world as separate from me, this perception is all that I know and therefore must be true or real. This reality is taken as self-evident and unquestionable. Therefore, what I know, or am taught and accept as being true, is patently what is and must be true, and those that might disagree with my perceptions and views are, at the very least, wrong, and at worst, evil.

Truth must fight falsehood, good must fight evil, and I must fight you, should your disagreement with me prove too problematic. It sounds to me like a solid recipe for suffering, and yet this is how we live. This is how we have always lived. It is the legacy of the human mind. Since the beginning of human consciousness, Man has felt himself to be separate from… something. He calls that something by a variety of names: God, Buddha, Allah, Great Spirit, Nature or perhaps even the Universe. And subsequently he has developed numerous religious beliefs to somehow maintain a connection with that which Zen insists he has never been separate from, not even for an instant. It requires a lot of energy to chase your own tail, and it's awfully frustrating - even my cat's given up on it.

The problem with words is that they are misleading, not in themselves, but in the way we interpret them. Words such as I, self, truth, delusion, reality…these are land mines we step on constantly. There is a Zen phrase which states, "Immeasurably great men are tossed about in the sea of words." A hundred people reading this can have a hundred different thoughts on what it must mean - and they can all be wrong. We can only see the world through the veils we've been given, both neurologically and culturally. We accept the veils so unconditionally that we don't even know we have them. But they distort our view and make it impossible to avoid the land mines which blow us to smithereens on a daily basis.

Zen is important because it gives us a way out of this horrible mess. It offers us a practice and realization to relax our grip on the delusions that bind us, on the delusions we ourselves have created.

The philosophy of Zen deals with two aspects of reality, known as the Absolute and the Relative. In Part One of this book, I will attempt to explain the vital importance of realizing the Absolute nature of our existence. It is important because, lacking an appreciation of it, we squander our lives chasing shadows, and this chase is an endless cause of suffering for ourselves and our world. I will use modern physics, specifically, relativity and quantum mechanics, as analogies to help explain what may initially seem contrary to common sense. But the problem with our common sense is that it is limited; it is truly unable to grasp the vast and unknowable functioning of the universe, yet our common sense takes itself and its blurred vision as an infallible and crystal clear observer of the Truth. Physics can help us because the two pillars of modern physics, relativity and quantum mechanics, meld perfectly with major concepts that Buddhism has addressed for 2,500 years.

First, in the case of Einstein's Relativity, we will see how the Absolute nature of light is an essential aspect of Einstein's discovery and also a critical metaphor in the mystical nature of Buddhist enlightenment and the philosophy that issues from it. Secondly, we will see how the study of quantum mechanics caused a direct challenge to the way Western logic had defined reality, a challenge that had long existed as part of Buddhist understanding. This exploration will be the defining quality of Part One, 'The Absolute'.

In Part Two, 'The Relative', we will deal with various aspects of our Relative world, the world we are all familiar with, and see whether or not our appreciation of the Absolute might give us a new way not only of looking at our world, but also of dealing with it. By that, I mean I want to investigate whether our suffering is an inevitable part of our existence or whether we may indeed have some power to deal with it more effectively, for the benefit of ourselves and others.

I came to Zen through a somewhat circuitous route. Although I began to study it when I was only 18, I spent a good 25 years pondering and practicing Zen before I finally felt truly comfortable with it. Although I lived in Japan and practiced in a lay Zen temple for almost five years in my youth, I've never been a monastic or a priest. I remain a layman to this day. I've been privileged to study with several outstanding teachers including Japan's great lay Zen Master, Osaka Koryu Roshi, Taizan Maezumi Roshi, one of the pioneers of Zen in the West, and finally the powerful and brilliant abbot of Zen Mountain Center, Charles Tenshin Fletcher Roshi, the author of *The Way of Zen*. I received Dharma Transmission from Tenshin Roshi in 2003, authorizing me to teach Zen in the White Plum lineage. Not only that, but my lovely and talented wife, Nicolee McMahon Roshi, a Dharma successor of Maezumi Roshi, has opened my eyes to a variety of gems, all sparkling and wonderful to behold.

Never having been a monastic, I've had to make my own way in the world. I've worked as a house painter, an actor, and after returning from Japan I became a U.S. Navy fighter pilot, flying F-14s off the deck of the *USS Nimitz* and graduated from the now famous Topgun (The Navy Fighter Weapons School). I also became a husband and a proud father. Currently I'm a commercial airline pilot. I played football and ran track in my youth, got a black belt in karate, and I still consider myself an avid surfer and golfer.

I relay all this merely to elucidate the fact that I'm not a Zen professional, and that perhaps is my only asset as a teacher of Zen. I'm not a professor of philosophy, I have no doctorate and I'm not a therapist. I'm just like you, an average U.S. citizen. I don't hang around with spiritual people, and most of my friends and co-workers have no knowledge of my place in American Zen, nor would they care. But this has also been an advantage for me, for I've been able to view a large cross-section of Americans for many years and see what makes them tick.

Americans in Zen are generally liberal and well-educated. Most pilots are conservative and don't care much for advanced learning, except in technology perhaps. Most Zen students are scholarly and introspective. Karate men, pilots and surfers are generally outgoing, confident, aggressive and occasionally drunk and obnoxious. (Or maybe that's just me.)

My years in Japan taught me a great deal about how the Japanese see themselves and the world, especially those involved in Zen. They honor tradition and place great emphasis on self-effacement. Americans like to stand out, or at least stand up and be counted. Individual rights are the bedrock of our democracy, and the primacy of the individual is paramount. In Japan, the social nexus is primary and individual rights are not clearly appreciated nor understood.

What I've just said may sound simplistic and stereotypical, yet stereotypes arise precisely because they are easy to understand and generally felt to be true. I certainly don't believe stereotypes to be necessarily true in individual cases, but at times they can provide a good general background for discussion. (I dare my fighter pilot friends to prove they've never been drunk and obnoxious.)

In this book, I will attempt to corral all this experience, from Topgun fighter pilots to Zen Masters, from surf bums to Einstein, and present a case for the importance of Zen and its teaching that can be seen in the broad areas covered by this book. It's a journey I will try to make engaging, even funny, while dealing seriously with issues as small as the quantum and as large as the universe; as silly as my old cat and as profound as enlightenment.

I'll do my best but I don't expect this book to be clear to everyone. It's very difficult to explain the truth of Zen, and that's why traditionally Zen Masters don't even try. They merely prod their students in the right direction until they see it for themselves. But in the end, if this book confuses you, I've probably done a decent job, because confusion can help free you from the cells of your own certainty.

PART ONE

THE ABSOLUTE

Chapter One

TOPGUN ZEN
The Importance of the Journey

What's the point of such a wide-ranging book? What's the connection between Topgun and Zen? From Topgun to Zen, and everything in between, we often suffer not because we are evil or unenlightened, but because we can easily fail to appreciate subtle truths of a reality that the conscious intellect vainly attempts to fix, solidify and hold fast. Simply put, this tension causes suffering.

The riddle of suffering is vast and intricate and does not succumb to simple answers. My early Zen practice taught me how the mind can trick us when we're caught in the endless waves it can churn. But flying in the Navy taught me something else…how we can suffer absent any conscious sin, how life can reach out to nail us, like an unseen enemy missile, especially when our intentions are clouded by misinformation and our activity arises from ignorance of natural law.

If I hold to negative thought patterns and identify with conceptual structures of who I am, I can easily suffer as a result. If I am dehydrated yet drink only coffee, I've compounded my problem because coffee is a diuretic. And if I believe it's an enemy in front of me and squeeze off a missile, but in reality it's my wingman that I've subsequently shot down, I create waves of pain and suffering that extend, literally, forever.

Suffering is a problem, a dilemma, a riddle. It's the most compelling challenge of life. Its cause is forever in motion, its answer real, yet elusive. Its challenge and its response can be found in every facet of the life we live. This book contains the various avenues I've walked that presented this challenge in different forms, and also deals with facets of our existence that are often ignored when dealing with the riddle of suffering.

From Childhood to Zen

I was a middle class kid growing up in Southern California. I attended a very small, private boys' school until 8th grade. It was a throwback to the 19th century, one little schoolhouse with kids from 3rd through 8th grade in the one small classroom all learning the same subjects from a stern headmaster. We studied Shakespeare, Latin, French, Spanish, algebra and geometry, to name a few. It was quite advanced for its time. Then I went to Catholic high school. That's where I learned about suffering.

Not because of the Catholic education per se. It was the girls. I made my acquaintance with suffering as a response to lost love. Nothing special. It happens every day. It doesn't seem like something that would make one become a Buddhist. But aren't there plenty of movies about jilted men joining foreign legions? I joined a foreign religion instead.

She was a cheerleader, as well as an athlete, a brain and a virgin; she was the beloved of God, the senior class and me. She was my first love, the most important woman of my early life (outside my mother) and the person my whole existence spun around and shot off in another direction, the plot point of my personal history.

There is something eternally compelling about first love. For me it was the first realization of the 'other', if you will, a breaking through of the shell of self that had been carefully constructed from childhood. It was a yearning, a reaching out to an attraction that was as unexplainable as it was undeniable, the compulsion and obsession so overwhelming that my life, my mind, were no longer mine to control, if they ever were in the first place. The experience awakened me to a feeling of such exuberance and joy as I'd never known before, like opening the doors to a powerful, cool and clear wind that blows through the house with a freshness of rebirth and endless possibility. And it also laid me open and naked before the inevitable realization that all things are fleeting, a lesson in pain I've never forgotten.

I had been a good Catholic, even an altar boy who feared the Devil and the wages of sin. But after the cheerleader dumped me, I turned away from the God of my fathers. I turned to the ways of the hippie, long hair and free love. You name it, I tried it, and it was great. But concurrently with the loss of love and the trial run at experimental release, I stumbled upon Zen. I can still remember reaching down to pick up a book from my brother's bed called *The Gospel According to Zen*. And as I write this chapter, over 35 years since that day, that small book of Zen stories sits next to me on my desk. It was the first book I had ever read from cover to cover without stopping. Somewhere in those wonderful stories I found, or at least fantasized I'd found, men who were enlightened, confident in themselves, and serene through all their ills. That's what I wanted for myself. I did not want to go through life hurt, confused, and vulnerable to women, to life, "to the slings and arrows of outrageous fortune". I was not focused on Buddhist compassion as such, but on a mind that had freed itself from the snares of intellectual and emotional hang-ups…powerful, indeed dominant, over life's vagaries. No more suffering. Such are the fairy tales of youth.

Over the next two years, the question of Zen and its relation to the belief structure I'd inherited would not let me rest. It seemed as if every waking moment I was compelled to investigate the concepts I'd been given against the new ones I was learning. I read Aldous Huxley's *The Doors of Perception* and fantasized about acid. The experience sounded wonderful, blissful, beyond doubt and desire. I thought the experience must be the Zen enlightenment of which I had read. But I felt if I could only get enlightened the real way, through Zen meditation, I could feel that way forever. But after two years of this intense personal questioning, I felt emptied. One by one I'd discarded the beliefs I'd grown up with and was left with nothing onto which I could hold. It was a scary and lonely feeling. It was then that I took up the practice of zazen, determined to push forward and not return to the place from which I had come.

I was also practicing karate at the time. I wanted to get strong and I wanted to get clear. For me, the Rinzai sect of Zen was just what the doctor ordered. I believed that its traditional affiliation with the martial arts and its emphasis on mental focus and clarity was my ticket to an experience of life beyond the muddled pain…and away I went.

Zen in Japan
I found my way to Japan through an education abroad program from the University of California at Santa Barbara.

With Asian Studies as my major and an emphasis on Japan, I had some solid Japanese language study behind me. Maezumi Roshi in Los Angeles had given me the address of a lay Zen temple in Japan called Hannya Dojo where he himself had lived and practiced as a teenager. So, it was in the fall of 1973 that I walked the narrow streets of Kichijoji, a suburb of Tokyo, and found the Hannya Dojo. Osaka Koryu Roshi was a Rinzai Zen Master in the Inzan lineage, only eight generations distant from the great Master Hakuin himself (1687-1768) who revitalized Zen for the modern era.

In Koryu Roshi, I found a master who met my expectations, strong and clear-eyed, and yet who was gentle. He and the members of his school were very kind to me, allowing me to live and practice there after only six months training. In the 50-year history of that school, I am the only foreigner who ever lived there for any length of time. I suppose it's my only claim to fame in Zen.

It was all a great adventure for me. Although not monastic, the life was one of a Zen temple. Up early every morning for zazen, and again in the evening. Dokusan (interview) twice a day with the master, all in Japanese. It was a great challenge…great fun. Immersing myself in the language and customs at the Hannya Dojo, I began to lose touch with English. At the end of my stay I was even dreaming in Japanese.

Koan study in Zen (explained in more detail in the next chapter) is efficacious on many levels, not the least of which is focusing the mind and breaking through conceptual structures that constrict our experience of life. The process was often trying, indeed excruciating. I remember working on the koan Mu during the Rohatsu sesshin of 1974. An important part of koan practice is the personal one-on-one interviews the master holds with the student called dokusan. Roshi sternly rang me out of the dokusan room time after time. I came to an impasse. The fatigue of the schedule, the stern and uncompromising master, and the pain of long sitting were getting to me. No matter what I did, no matter what I said, I couldn't pass. I even refused to get into the dokusan line once and was dragged off my seat by a senior student and ordered to go. But in the end I passed.

Over the years I was there I felt I had made good progress on my quest. I was also able to practice karate and by the end of my stay in Japan I had a black belt, confidence in my physical skills and confidence in the clear mind I had worked to achieve through years of meditation and koan practice with a true master.

After almost five years in Japan, I was ready to come home. My teacher, Koryu Roshi, had fallen ill and had stopped teaching and I felt I had come to the end of something. I had learned much, more even than I felt possible before I went there. But now it was time to go. But where?

It was my 26th birthday, and I was riding a train to downtown Tokyo to teach English at the Pioneer Electric Corporation. It was one of the two jobs I had in Japan. The other was acting - that was the fun one. I remember how excited I was when I went to my first job to act in a TV drama with no less than Toshiro Mifune himself, the samurai hero from such famous films as *The Seven Samurai* and *Yojimbo*. He was the most famous Japanese actor in the West, appearing with Lee Marvin in Hell in the Pacific, with James Garner in Grand Prix, with Richard Chamberlain in Shogun, and in other films.

Now, toward the end of my stay in Japan, I needed something, some job to go home to. I can still remember riding that train downtown and thinking about acting as a career. Too difficult, I thought. I had friends who were trying to break into Hollywood with little success. Besides, I wanted something real, not make-believe. There was a newsworthy event that had taken place a year and a half earlier. A Russian pilot named Viktor Belenko had defected, flying his Mig-25 Foxbat into Hakodate in Japan. At that time, I was actually working on a Hong Kong film being shot in Tokyo called Foxbat. I was a stand-in and stunt man for the American actor, Henry Silva, who was playing an agent involved in the Belenko affair.

This film started me thinking. Why don't I become an American fighter pilot? My father had been a Navy pilot during World War II. Why not? This may seem strange to many readers. Why would a Zen Buddhist student suddenly shift gears and want to become a fighter pilot? But the Rinzai sect of Zen, in which I was practicing at the time, had a long relationship with the Japanese martial philosophy. Since the time of Zen's introduction to Japan from China in the 12th and 13th centuries, many famous samurai took up the practice of Zen as a means to hone the spirit behind the skills they possessed. They sensed that Zen's emphasis on direct experience and mental composure even in the face of life's most pressing dilemma, i.e., death, could do much to aid their efforts. This philosophy also appealed greatly to me at the time because, as a young man, I felt that courage and confidence arising from true understanding could make me the man I wanted to be. Such was my thinking in those days. Rinzai Zen…karate…what a perfect combination for a fighter pilot!

From Zen to Topgun

So back I came to the USA, applied to the Navy and entered Aviation Officer Candidate School barely one month shy of reaching the maximum age limit of 27. At the completion of basic flight training, I received orders to the F-14 RAG (Replacement Air Group) to train in the Tomcat.

In my fleet squadron, the VF-41 Black Aces, they gave me the call sign "Monk", in mock honor of my Zen training in Japan. What fun it all was! Zooming and booming through the skies with a great group of guys in the finest Navy fighter jet of its day; it was a time of dogfights over the ocean, dogfights over the desert, going from supersonic speeds just above the waves or sand dunes and zooming up to zero airspeed above 40,000 feet…even chasing Col. Khadaffi's Migs around the Gulf of Sidra. And after a year and a half, I was selected to attend the Navy's famous Power Projection course at Topgun. It was quite an exhilarating time!

What a boost for a Buddhist ego. It's funny how easily the fragile ego is impressed, taking even the slightest encouragement as rationale to goose-step its way through the arch of petty triumphs, offering a little flag and a swift kick in the pants for all onlookers to agree and waive and cheer.

All my life I've suffered from high self-esteem. You see, what I perceived as success in Zen actually enlarged my ego.

It did not shatter it. A little wisdom is a dangerous thing and, of course, the ego of the fighter pilot is legend. Actually, people would at times compliment me, saying, in effect, "For a fighter pilot, you're quite humble," and they really meant it. But if I wasn't bragging, it was only because deep inside I held myself in such high esteem that the availability, or lack, of accolades from others meant little to me. I was my own ideal.

You can imagine where that led. It doesn't help much in relationships - with women, with children, with parents and even, at times, with friends equally as satisfied with themselves. So eventually the heel of Achilles was pierced once more, and he fell, his armor clanging around him as it cracked and broke on the windy plains of Troy. Sometimes a warrior loves only himself, cares so much for himself that strength is the only thing he desires. Strength so that he will never lose, never hurt, and never die.

From Topgun to Zen

From the time I left Japan, I had always intended to return to Zen one day. I even tried to maintain a practice by traveling from my Navy base in Virginia Beach to Bernie Tetsugen Glassman Roshi's Zen Center in New York on occasion. He was a dharma successor of Maezumi Roshi's and I'd known him since my first Zen retreat in 1972. But it was too much to combine that with the hectic 'here today gone tomorrow' life of a fighter squadron so I had to give up the formal Zen training.

But the tatters of my personal life forced me to find a way back to Zen in 1993 where I reacquainted myself with Maezumi Roshi in Los Angeles. I was determined to finish the koan practice I began in Japan twenty years earlier and to learn why, after what I considered spiritual and personal achievement in many ways, I still managed to make a mess of things and find suffering anew.

And that really is the whole point of this book. The possibility of suffering lies deep in every fiber of our being, like a cancer just waiting to emerge. Simple answers usually only result in more suffering. We need to approach it with a fine scalpel, not a sledgehammer. We can easily throw the baby out with the bathwater.

You can meditate in your cave for twenty years, attain enlightenment, and still suffer from emotional baggage that remains untouched. You can be the greatest warrior in the world and perish from the bite of a tiny bug.

In every realm of human endeavor, we can find the challenge of suffering. We find suffering at home, at work, in love and in war. Buddhism's resolution to our suffering can extend broadly into most avenues of our lives. Yet it is not science, and cannot tell us how to build an energy-efficient car, fly to the moon or understand the electron. And this scientific understanding also has spiritual implications. Poor understanding of natural law can cause suffering, as in pollution unchecked or sickness untreated, and the pains of physical existence can often lead to spiritual doubt, which in turn can lead to more suffering.

Scientific knowledge can ease human suffering, but without wisdom, the benefits may be short-lived. In Buddhism, this wisdom is prajna, a non-dualistic appreciation of existence. Knowledge of the natural world can help release us from mythologies that may bind us, and wisdom of the true nature of our existence can motivate us toward realistic solutions to the riddles of pain and suffering we all share.

This is why I've addressed such wide-ranging topics as mysticism, science, air combat and daily life. When we ignore aspects of our existence, we suffer from that lack of attention. We find our riddle in the monastery, in the laboratory, in our relationships, in war, in peace and in the conduct of our lives. The riddle is in our bodies, in our minds and in our hearts. But we do have the capacity to affect the riddle. This is our challenge.

Chapter Two

THE TEACHING OF EMPTINESS
The Importance of Mu

As I stated in the Introduction, we are born in this world, and trained to function in it, with several delusions accepted as fact. More precisely, we accept without question the often limited consciousness our brains produce as an absolute fact, i.e., that what we perceive is indeed the truth, that what we know is undeniable. We conclude, therefore, that there is an objective reality upon which all sane people can agree, and that other views must be incorrect, foolish, stupid or evil. This dynamic arises from the solid and entrenched feeling of the individual self, the ego, as separate from the rest of existence. This is the basis of dualistic thinking, that the separate self is set apart from life and must continually deal with it as an opponent, sometimes easily and favorably, and at times angrily and antagonistically.

Many beliefs that arise from this dualistic premise, both religious and personal, accept this basic fallacy as truth, and are, from the Zen point of view, limited and ultimately misguided. This fallacy compels us to deal with that which is outside us, and greater than us, in an almost medieval, serf-like fashion. We must prostrate, obey and fear the repercussions of this Other, whether it be called God, Allah, the Universe or what have you. It is, in the end, what is out to *get us* and this limitation can exacerbate a basic cause of suffering. It suffuses us with doubt about our place in the cosmos, and this doubt is a tension that will not release its perennial hold. Thoreau echoed this sentiment when he said that most men lead lives of quiet desperation. And sometimes, as we all know, not so quiet.

Contemplative Buddhists meditate. That is their practice. In Zen, this meditation is called zazen, literally, "seated meditation". It is here we attempt to bore through, or let go of, our normal dualistic consciousness and settle into something more, into another aspect of mind that all humans possess, yet are generally blind to. We practice zazen to plumb the depths of our own minds, see through the illusory concepts that bind us and to realize the truth of something Buddhism calls Emptiness.

The two most prominent schools of Zen Buddhism that survive to this day are the Soto and the Rinzai sects. In the Soto School, the direct meditation practice of shikantaza, or just sitting, has traditionally been emphasized. In the Rinzai School, meditation has traditionally been augmented by the use of koans. The student will be given a koan upon which to meditate...a question that must be answered. The term literally means "public case", a record from Zen Buddhist history of a story or anecdote that drives us to the heart of Zen. Although in this sense they are similar to Bible stories used in church sermons, their often illogical nature and bizarre exhortations can be quite confusing and even shocking to the uninitiated.

But koans are illogical only when viewed solely by man's dualistic intellect. When viewed from that deeper place, often called the Zen eye, they make perfect sense. They express the wisdom inherent in all of us, a wisdom that often remains obscured beneath layers, indeed millennia, of conditioning.

It is the goal of Zen practice to peel back these layers to reveal our True Nature. In Buddhism, this wisdom is called prajna, and it is revealed to the practitioner upon his or her insight into the reality of Emptiness, originally called in Sanskrit, Shunyata.

The teaching of Emptiness is Buddhism's gift to human understanding. And the invitation of Zen practice is to realize this Emptiness, and to then integrate that understanding and the compassion that arises from it into our daily lives.

The following is often the first koan used in traditional Zen practice, and is found in a Zen text called the Mumonkan, or Gateless Gate:

A monk asked Joshu in all earnestness, "Does a dog have the Buddha-nature or not?"

Joshu said, "Mu!"

The Zen student will mediate on this koan, sometimes for several years, before coming to even a glimpse of its meaning. I had a friend once who happened to stumble onto my old copy of R. H. Blyth's translation of the Mumonkan, who read this case and almost died laughing. "Joshu said, 'Mu'? What the hell is that?" he laughed. It's a very appropriate question. What the hell is Mu anyway? It reminds me of a Monte Python movie, *The Life of Brian*, where the three Wise Men come to the wrong house in search of the baby Jesus and give gold, frankincense and myrrh to the baby Brian. Brian's mother is grateful, yet stupefied, and in the end asks "What the hell is myrrh, anyway?"

At first the case makes perfect sense to us in English. Does a dog have Buddha-nature? In other words, does even a lowly dog have something called Buddha-nature that raises it above the mundane? We might ask in a more Western sense, does God care for a dog as he does humankind? Does the rain truly fall evenly on the just and the unjust?

Traditional Christian thinking argues that Man alone is preeminent on Earth, but Buddhism does not have an authoritarian figure that created Man. Historically, Buddhism taught that all beings are equal and none high and none low, but Zen Master Joshu challenges even this when he responds to the question with a simple answer, "Mu". This answer is often taken as a direct negation, or "No" in response to the monk's question. Is Joshu merely denying a basic Buddhist concept, i.e., the equality of all life?

A longer version of this case can be found in another Zen text, the *Shoyoroku*, or *Book of Equanimity*. In that version, the monk asks basically the same question twice, and gets two different answers..."Yes" one time, and "No" the next. But the characters for what we translate as, "Yes" and "No" are pronounced in Japanese, 'U ' (ooh) and 'Mu' (mooh) respectively. These can also be translated as existence (U) and non-existence (Mu), or being and nothingness.

The word *Mu* has no meaning for us in the English language, whereas to a Japanese monk it means a great deal. Mu, or Nothingness, means something, although initially the student may not know what. It rings a bell in the psyche, whereas for a Western Zen student Mu is just a sound. The case can be dealt with simply as a negative response to the monk's question. In that case, the Zen practitioner will learn a basic Zen lesson as he struggles with the dilemma of what seems to be a great Zen Master denying a basic Buddhist tenet. But there is more here to appreciate.

Meditation on Mu is often thought of as a mantra-like technique. The student may mediate silently on Mu and become absorbed in that one thought or sound. There are several levels of Buddhist understanding that such meditation can produce. Initially, the student may supplant his or her perennial thought patterns which spiral around a concept and feeling of self, or ego, and arrive at a state where Mu has replaced the intermediate *I*. This *I* would normally, as a conditioned response, feel the necessity to label and categorize whatever it experiences all through the endlessly convoluted filter of the conditioned self.

We are all playwrights, constantly writing the story of life, concocting an endless drama with ourselves as the central character, the star of the show. And we are always amazed at the poor reviews we often receive. It's like telling a joke. One person may laugh at it and another may frown. Why does one person applaud my story and another one criticize it? It is simply because most of what we call life, or reality, is just that - just a story written by the self, unaware of its own self-imposed limitations. It is unavoidably different from someone else's story, which is likewise limited by its own special movement through space and time.

The word *Mu* cuts through and even replaces this normal seat of consciousness, which is dominated by an ego concept, and inherited and cultivated over much time. The ensuing experience of phenomena in its pure state, without self-centered conceptual interference, is termed in Buddhism Suchness, or Thusness.

Just This is a favorite phrase of Zen Masters everywhere, and attempts to point to the profound nature of the present moment when the muddying dysfunction of the intellect finally lets go of its stranglehold. This experience in itself is quite illuminating, and shows us finally how we fail to grasp the truth of things because we are constantly stuck in our heads with the stories we are spinning about reality, when in fact the reality itself has already vanished. As my grandfather would often say "…a half hour late and a dollar short!" A Buddhist master could not have said it better.

But practicing with *Mu* where the notion of self, indeed the actual feeling of self, can drop off and cease its constant interpretation of the world for a time, could be criticized by some as just a sort of brainwashed state brought about by the continual repetition of the word *Mu*. Such criticism is partially fair, but ignores the fact that, lacking an extraordinary effort, even if somewhat contrived, it is rare that one can break the hold of a conscious mind we take for granted, even idolize. That is, until it leads us to suffering.

Still, the foregoing description of the practice with *Mu*, which can produce a profound shift in consciousness in the student, is still far from the mind of Joshu.

In his commentary on this case, Mumon, the Zen Master who originally compiled the text, says "Do not construe Mu as nothingness and do not conceive it in terms of existence or non-existence." According to another translation it reads,

"Do not form a nihilistic conception of vacancy, or a relative conception of 'has' or 'has not'." That is because the concept of existence always implies self-nature, or the holding of phenomena as a separate and identifiable construct from which we build our human reality, and the concept of non-existence implies mere absence of being and vacuity. Joshu's Mu is neither of these.

Yasutani Roshi, a famous Zen Master of the 20th century, and my own great-grandfather in the Dharma, comments on this case in Philip Kapleau's book, *The Three Pillars of Zen*. He says, "[Mu]… is itself Buddha-nature…the retort 'Mu!' exposes and at the same time fully thrusts Buddha-nature before us." He also says that the substance of this Buddha or Dharma-nature is ku, shunyatta. "Now ku is not mere Emptiness. It is that which is living, dynamic, devoid of mass, unfixed beyond individuality or personality - the matrix of all phenomena. Here we have the fundamental principle or doctrine or philosophy of Buddhism."

I once asked Maezumi Roshi if there were any difference between Mu, or Nothingness, and Ku, or Emptiness. He said that was really a question for scholars, but that Mu was a Taoist expression already in use in China when Buddhism and its teaching of Emptiness entered the country around 500 CE. Chinese Buddhists merely borrowed the Taoist term to express the Dharma and make it more palatable to the Chinese mind. Therefore - and this is the important point - for purposes of this koan, Mu and Ku are synonymous.

The realization of Emptiness (Ku) is the goal of this koan, and it is at one and the same time the world in which we all live and the world which most of humanity has never even dreamed of. The contemplation of Mu is perhaps a mantra-like device, even better, perhaps, for an English-speaking person because it is devoid of meaning, merely a sound, and the student will not get caught up in theorizing about Nothingness or Emptiness. Yet what Joshu is pointing to is nothing other than this Emptiness.

Buddhist teachers in various schools or sects will speak of Emptiness in slightly different ways. Some use the term as synonymous with impermanence, the teaching that all phenomena are empty of self-nature, i.e., that they are merely combinations of various forces which coalesce momentarily to produce what we call reality. But the key here is that while Emptiness is indeed a Buddhist teaching and understanding, on its deepest level it is a psychophysical realization where our existential doubt is wiped away faster than dust from a windshield. It is this very world perceived from the timeless standpoint of what Zen Master Bankei calls the Unborn, where all phenomena, i.e., everything that you can see, hear, smell, taste, touch or be enlightened or deluded about, is nothing more than the temporary and fleeting manifestation of this same Emptiness. It is formless, timeless and full of vitality.

Zen Masters often ask, "Mountains and rivers, where do they come from?" The fact is that they neither come nor go. Their essential nature is the same as yours or mine. It is this Emptiness, this pulsating energy of essential wisdom that is all of life.

What we can see, hear and know is mere appearance, a temporary construct where the energy appears solidified. It is like a tornado where the air is spinning fast enough to appear as a funnel, but when the energy dissipates it becomes invisible air once more.

So is our life, from the highest mountain to the smallest drop of water, from every enlightenment to every delusion, nothing but Emptiness itself...Emptiness appearing as form. Einstein voiced a similar view from the world of physics when he said that the universe really is nothing but energy, and all the matter in it merely condensed energy.

From the standpoint of this realization, all the great traditions of mankind, all the artistic, athletic, political, technical and social achievements of human history, and even the enlightenment of Buddha himself is of no more importance than the mere raising of a finger into the air. It rises from Emptiness, returns to Emptiness, is itself from beginning to end nothing but unfathomable and ineffable Emptiness.

In Buddhism we talk often of the unfixed nature of reality, and this is a critical aspect of its teaching. From the relative side, Emptiness functions relatively. Yet from the absolute side, Emptiness is eternally present, bright and serene, without opinion or direction, motion or limit, expression or response. Undivided and undisturbed, it is, as Maezumi Roshi once said, "Totally impersonal, and always at peace." One of the ancestors of the Soto School, Master Keizan, wrote, "It is clear, alert and always bright."

To understand and appreciate this requires what Buddhism calls *enlightenment*, or realization. Shaku Soen Roshi, considered the epitome of a Zen prodigy in Japan in the early part of the 20th century, said that enlightenment is, "…seeing the lamp of eternity shining through the mist of transiency." I love his expression and I would add that enlightenment also means realizing that this lamp of eternity shines forth *as* the mists of *our own* transiency. Everything we are and everything we can experience is but a momentary flash of this shining light.

We often think of life as plodding along from moment to moment, but here we realize that there is really only *one moment*, a timeless moment, an eternal breath. It is here that Zen takes its place with the great religious traditions of mankind, for Joshu's Mu is none other than the *eye* of Meister Eckhart, and the Divine of St. John. It is the original face, the true home, the lap of salvation, the Face of God. The practice of *Mu* may lead to an understanding of Suchness, direct perception unclouded by the molasses of conceptual thinking, an appreciation of the Zen phrase *Just This*. It may also lead to what Zen calls the "dropping off of body and mind," where the walls of the individual self disintegrate like shattered glass, and only *one body* is experienced. This is fine as far as it goes, and would certainly be termed enlightenment as well. But Joshu's aim is nothing other than Mind Essence itself, undivided and eternal…beyond being and non-being, existence and non-existence, oneness, two-ness or anything else you can think of or experience. Beyond time itself, IT IS! This shining breath of shunyatta is ultimate reality, or what is called in Zen *the Absolute*. And once perceived, this realization enables us to release our conditioned grasp on this illusory world, which is finally seen for what it is. In the end, what we can know about the world, and our lives in it, are but the temporary and fleeting manifestations of something greater that we can only intuit. Physicists would call it *energy*, but in Zen, there is only *one body* functioning as this universe. Just *one* thing. It appears as mountains. It appears as clouds. It appears as thought. It appears as emotion. It appears as craving. It appears as aversion. It appears as enlightenment. It appears as delusion. *It* does not appear. And *it* does not disappear.

We begin to see ourselves as ghosts reaching out to grasp at other ghosts, often not realizing the empty nature of anything and everything. Life is seen as an exquisite mystery where all that we can feel and know is transparent and ephemeral, fading faster than a snowflake on warm ground, or a teardrop in the rain.

It is often said in Zen that the koan Mu is as impenetrable as an iron wall. But far from being an impenetrable iron wall that none or few can grasp, Mu is as flimsy as tissue paper, as limpid as a clear pool. Once you see it, you realize that even your own confusion and delusion is none other than Emptiness itself, as fleeting and free as the path of birds across the trackless sky.

So who truly realizes this? Who has had this wonderful experience? The answer is simple. No one! I've never had it. You've never had it. The great Zen Masters have never had it. Even Shakyamuni Buddha never had it. At this level, *it* experiences *itself*. Meister Eckhart said that, "...the Eye by which I see God is the same Eye by which God sees me." Zen Master Dogen said, "...only Buddha becomes Buddha."

Here the so-called self has truly dropped away, and the light shines forth of its own accord. Wherever you look, wherever you turn, nothing but Emptiness everywhere. What you see is empty, and what you see with is empty too. Subject and object are both empty.

Yamada Koun Roshi said that enlightenment is seeing the Emptiness of subject and object. And he might have added, the Emptiness of the experience, as well. For if it is true, it reveals itself as another of the fleeting empty experiences of life, impossible to hold on to, vanishing like a fog of breath from a silver tray.

Are you confused? That's it! Enlightened? Deluded? That's it! Beautiful? Ugly? Smart? Stupid? A master? A student? At one with the universe? Feeling separated? Try though you may you'll never find it...because you're never without it.

It's not only what you seek. IT'S WHAT SEEKS! It's what seeks and what finds. It's what doesn't seek and doesn't find. It's what seeks forever but never finds. It's what refuses to seek but stumbles onto somehow. See it once and it's seen forever.

So...does a dog have the Buddha-nature?? Joshu merely said "Mu!" And that one soft-spoken word has penetrated centuries of delusion. He's pointing the monk to the essential world in which there is no monk, no Joshu, no Buddha-nature, no dog. The monk *is* Buddha-nature, Joshu, too, the dog as well and the question itself. Buddha-nature *is* the monk's confusion and Joshu's certainty. It's all-inclusive and leaves nothing out.

I'm reminded of the case that comes at the end of one of Zen Master Dogen's great works called Genjo Koan. The monk asks the master if it's true that the nature of wind is permanent and pervades everywhere. The master says that it is true. The student then asks, "If it is true then why do you fan yourself?" The master replies that although the monk may realize that the nature of wind is permanent, he does not understand the meaning of its "pervading everywhere." The monk then asks, "Then what is the meaning of its pervading everywhere?" The master just fanned himself.

Everywhere means just that. EVERYWHERE! Into every nook and cranny of your confusion, anger, lust and pain it pervades. And also to your desire to rid yourself of these poisons.

Zen students often get stuck in their practice thinking that Zen is "Just This." That somehow concentration on the present moment and avoiding the trap of an overactive thought process is the final truth of Buddhism. But as an ancient Chinese Zen master, Yuan-Wu, pointed out, "The present moment is indeed the truth, but the truth is far beyond this present moment. Step back all the way and it's Just This perhaps. But when you get to the place where even This is not yet established, that's the place to do the work." That place is the Unborn Mind Essence of Joshu's Mu...an eternal flow in which there is absolutely no movement at all. Time within timelessness, movement within stasis.

We talk a lot about our attachments and our struggle for liberation, but can you show me how you are attached to anything right now? If you can't hold to anything, aren't you already free?

Liberation is not something we achieve; it's our birthright. And Emptiness, the wisdom of this universe, is what has given it to us. Our lives go from birth to death, pleasure to pain, delusion to enlightenment, and back again. No matter how hard you try and enslave yourself, you're free. For the dynamic of Emptiness in form, constant flow, is forever in action, in the ceaseless mutation of each moment.

That is why Buddhism calls phenomena illusory, because of its transparent and fleeting nature. If you say things exist, then show me something that exists. But if you pick up a stick and show it to me, isn't what you're showing me something totally different from what you initially perceived to pick up? Only inattention claims it to be the same thing. So then nothing exists? If that is so, where did the stick, you, me and the question itself come from?

All these categories bind us. We continually build little castles of certainty into which we cram life, and we lock ourselves in these little cells and wonder why it's so stuffy inside, and soon begin yelling for help, for freedom.

Mumon picked this koan as the first koan in his collection for a very good reason, for it is the first and last koan of Zen practice. It is said that he worked for six years on it and upon his realization wrote this poem:

>Mu! Mu! Mu! Mu! Mu! Mu!
>Mu! Mu! Mu! Mu! Mu! Mu!
>Mu! Mu! Mu! Mu! Mu! Mu!
>Mu! Mu!

This poem reveals the key to the koan itself, unhindered by anything, all-inclusive and pervasive. Were I to theorize in my head and philosophize for a hundred years about the meaning, I would not move one step closer to the truth of existence that Mumon reveals in his poem. But I want to emphasize that if I were to theorize for a hundred years, I would also not move one step away from it either.

On his deathbed, Mumon wrote:

> Emptiness is unborn
> Emptiness does not pass away.
> When you know emptiness
> You are not different from it.

At the end of his life, Mumon restated the essence of Joshu's Mu for posterity. This Emptiness is the eternal wellspring of all life. If you know Emptiness, you and it are not different. But even if you don't know it, you and Emptiness are still not different. For *not knowing* is nothing but Emptiness itself.

The human intellect doesn't just attempt to classify reality. It unconsciously ossifies it. The practice of *Mu* can help us break down this intricate web of delusion and allow the natural brilliance of Mind to shine forth, vital, unhindered and sublime.

Chapter Three

THE PRICE OF APPLES
THE IMPORTANCE OF PHYSICS

They say that when an apple fell on Sir Isaac Newton's head he discovered gravity. After reading the previous chapter, you might wonder what all this mystical nonsense might have to do with the price of that apple. What does all this talk of Emptiness have to do with my life, indeed, with reality?

My first exposure to modern physics came in my 8th grade science class. I'll never forget the first question on my final exam. It was, "Explain Einstein's theory of relativity as it relates to his famous equation Emc2." In 8th grade, no less! Since then, I've spent many years wondering exactly what it all meant and why I needed to waste so much valuable television time on this kind of homework.

Religion, especially in the mystical traditions like Zen, is thought of by some to be divorced from the so-called real world. Priests may talk of God in the West, or Buddha in the East, but isn't all this just ancestor worship by people too old-fashioned in their ways to appreciate the actual workings of the real world as taught by science? Aren't those in religion merely engaging in sedating the masses, as Marx thought, and in cahoots with those in power to make us useful tools for those who know the way in which the real world of power politics and big business works?

On the other side of this equation, we find those who criticize science. So what if Einstein showed that space and time are relative constructs? Science can tell us nothing about how to live a good life, a life of quality in which people can know how to deal with one another in ethical ways conducive to a harmonious society. And what can science do to salve my doubt about my place in the universe?

But I do not believe that science, and in our case, physics, is divorced from life, even a good life, at all, because much of human action is based upon what we understand to be true. As human beings, we act not only from biological necessity but also from what we know and what we are taught. But if what we know and what we are taught is grounded in mythology rather than fact, then our lives will inevitably suffer the consequences of that folly.

History gives us many examples of this harmful dynamic in action. From conquest to genocide, from Inquisitions to witch trials, countless innocent people have been put to death. And far from being justly punished, often their only crime was that they were women, foreigners, victims of intolerance, ill-founded public hysteria or mental illness.

And even now there continue to be religious prohibitions even against a variety of foods that are relatively harmless to humans when properly cooked. Such rules may have begun before the value of proper preparation was understood and many suffered illness or death by eating them. Yet the rules remain as part of a spiritual life.

In the absence of science, human beings have often suffered greatly from nothing more than mistaken ideas; ideas that have arisen from belief systems constructed to explain the world to a populace in fear of the unknown on one hand, and needing guidance, coordination and control on the other.

Since the 1970's, there have been a number of books and articles attempting to show the fascinating correlation of traditional Buddhist philosophy to modern physics. Works that immediately come to mind are Fritjof Capra's, *The Tao of Physics* and Gary Zukav's, *The Dancing Wu Li Masters*. Both remain popular books, especially for Buddhists, as they attempt to relate how the two pillars of modern physics, Einstein's theories of relativity and quantum mechanics, point to aspects of reality that Buddhism has espoused for 2,500 years, aspects that have remained generally unknown or illogical to the Western mind.

I have heard physicists criticize such popular works as fanciful and overstated. As a small example, what is known in physics as *entanglement* is a phenomenon where our measurement of a particle's properties at one location will immediately affect its twin or sister particle at another location, no matter where that twin is in the universe, even perhaps light-years away. This bizarre effect, thought impossible by Einstein, has been proven experimentally many times in the last thirty years. But some physicists would criticize a Buddhist attempt to say this then proves that the universe is 'one and undivided' as an exaggeration, because such phenomena are only seen in highly controlled laboratory experiments, and their entangled results are easily interfered with. But as Sigmund Freud said, "Analogies prove nothing, that is quite true, but they make one feel more at home." And if Zen is anything at all, it's a practice designed to make us feel more at home, with a sense of comfort in the cosmos. I don't take modern physics as proof of my philosophy, but I do feel there are wonderful analogies to be found in the understandings of modern physics that can help us in our quest to disentangle the human mind from the delusory knots of its own creation.

Actually, I've always found Buddhist philosophy easier to swallow than the physics, which, until recently, captivated but confused me beyond measure. But after some years of serious study, coupled with the help of some modern physicists who've done an outstanding job of explaining their work to the layman, I believe the basic findings are accessible to almost anyone who takes the time to step through the progress that modern physics has brought to humankind. The various aspects of relativity and quantum mechanics, if taken out of the context of the history of physics, can seem perplexing at best. However, when viewed through the clarifying lens of its own history, these modern marvels reveal some astonishing truths that had remained hidden to our normal or common sense outlook on reality, but had been suggested by Buddhist understanding for millennia.

The advent of science often ran counter to long-accepted notions of the world, and in so doing, caused great upheaval. For purposes of this book, the most important advances were the study of motion and the Copernican Revolution, Einstein's Relativity and quantum mechanics. I will attempt to point to the gist of these remarkable leaps in human understanding without getting the reader bogged down in the details. For those interested in a more detailed description, I'd recommend Professor Richard Wolfson's lectures from the Teaching Company, "Einstein's Relativity and the Quantum Revolution: Modern Physics for Non-Scientists", and Brian Green's wonderful book, *The Fabric of the Cosmos*.

The Study of Motion and the Copernican Revolution

Since the time of the ancient Greeks, the study of physics has been about the study of motion and about the motion of objects. Our lives are made up, basically, of space and time. We exist in and experience life as three dimensions of space (length, width and height), and one dimension of time.

Buddhism generally talks about eight consciousnesses. The first six are familiar to everyone. They are eye consciousness, ear consciousness, nose consciousness, tongue consciousness, body consciousness (or sensation) and mind consciousness (or the intellect). What we experience in life, what we can see, hear, smell, taste, touch and even think about is drawn from a fabric of matter and energy woven through this space and time. According to physics, in order to understand it we need to understand motion and its laws because all that we are and all that we know moves through this space and time. This then was the study of classical mechanics.

The first question the Greeks dealt with was, "What is the most natural state of motion?" For them, the most natural state of motion was to be at rest close to the center of the earth. An object at rest tended to remain at rest unless acted upon by an agent. A push was required to move an object, and this push was required to keep an object in motion. (Note: A clearly defined notion of force was not developed until Sir Isaac Newton.) All this seemed self-evident and undeniable; one need merely to observe the world carefully.

One more thing seemed self-evident to the Greeks; that the earth was the center of the universe.

There were some astronomers, Greek and Arab and perhaps others, who questioned this view of the cosmos, yet Geocentrism became so strong in the West that to question it became tantamount to heresy in the Catholic Church.

But despite all the pressure to conform to long accepted views, Nicolaus Copernicus published his refutation of Geocentrism in 1543. His *On the Revolution of the Heavenly Spheres* set forth his belief that the sun, and not the Earth, was at the center of the cosmos. Some say he published this earth-shattering work after his death to avoid a confrontation with the Church and perhaps a sentence of death at the stake.

But shortly thereafter, Galileo came along and, with the use of a telescope, had the gall to actually prove that Copernicus was correct. Brilliant though Galileo was, he was not smart enough or prudent enough to wait until he was dead to prove it. And, as you may have imagined, it didn't take long for the Inquisition to come knocking to question him about his "wrong views". He was spared the ultimate penalty and instead given a sentence of life imprisonment in the house of his friend and pupil, Ferdinando II de' Medici. The Church, I suppose, was trying to show that it was not, after all, unreasonable.

The discovery that the earth was not the center of the cosmos became known as the Copernican Revolution. It destroyed the idea that our planet Earth held a special place as the center, the focal point of the universe. It was merely another place in the cosmos, no better or worse than any other. And from your own experience you can imagine the shock of it. We all think we're the center of the universe. Every child thinks the world revolves around him or her. Every race thinks it's the chosen people. The Chinese ideogram used to identify their country translates as something like Central Kingdom or Middle Nation. We like to be the center of attention so much that our ancient cosmologies actually defined us as that very thing, the center of God's attention. It's fun to be the life of the party.

But somehow the Church felt threatened by the idea that we were not the center of God's cosmos. The terrible fragmentation of doubts that could arise from that idea was endless. Were we then *not* made in His image? Was then Mary possibly *not* a virgin? Was the authority of the Church just a ruse? Even today there are fundamentalists in a variety of religions that feel that all of human suffering issues from the simple fact that their particular bible is not literally believed and followed.

But Galileo is important to us for other reasons, as well. He redefined motion. He showed that natural motion was not to be at rest as the Greeks believed, but that natural motion was uniform motion in a straight line, that is, motion in a straight line at constant speed. This is the law of inertia that is attributed to both Galileo and Newton. Imagine Galileo's genius that he could accurately imagine, as a thought experiment, an object like a small ball being pushed, and absent the frictional effects of outside agents, continuing along in the direction and velocity of its initial motion, quite literally, forever!

But Galileo also tried to show us the relative nature of motion. That is, whether you are at rest or in motion is totally dependent on your frame of reference. There is no experiment that you can do in physics that can establish something called rest or motion without reference to something else. For example, I'm sitting in my chair, at rest relative to my computer. But we all know that the earth's surface to which I'm attached is moving relative to the sun, therefore so am I. Even though I may be flying in an F-14 and am moving very rapidly relative to the earth's surface, I'm at rest relative to the Radar Intercept Officer (RIO) in the back seat.

In the days when I flew F-14s for a living, people would occasionally ask me, often wide-eyed and excited, "What's it like to go supersonic?" I hated to disappoint them as I replied, "Kind of like standing here talking to you." The great speed of Mach 1 was certainly exciting if I was flying low to a desert floor or sea surface where the reference point of sand dunes or wave tops screamed past my vision like a Star Wars scene of Luke Skywalker jumping to warp speed. But once a steady state (or uniform) speed of Mach 1 was reached at high altitude, there was little to no reference for feeling the speed. And that's the whole point - without a reference point, uniform motion and rest are indistinguishable.

And the important thing about all this is that the laws of physics work perfectly well for all these different situations. If I hold my pen up before me and let go of it, it will fall into my lap, whether I'm sitting in front of my computer or flying along at a uniform speed of Mach 1, the speed of sound. Remember, we're talking only of uniform motion now, not accelerated motion. That is a different topic Einstein covered in his General Theory of Relativity published in 1915. Uniform motion means that whatever object we are discussing, from pens to planes to you or me, is neither accelerating nor decelerating. Therefore, uniform motion and rest are equivalent.

And the wonderful revelation about all this is what has become known as the Principle of Galilean Relativity that states that the laws of motion are valid for all observers in uniform motion in any frame of reference. Remember this well and repeat it for it will become a central feature of our philosophical discussions later on. The laws of motion are valid for *all observers* in uniform motion in *any* frame of reference.

Sir Isaac Newton, born the year of Galileo's death under house arrest in 1642, used Galileo's ideas in formulating his laws of motion that very clearly showed and mathematically predicted the movement of objects in the universe, from little apples to large planets.

We call them the "laws" of physics precisely because they work well everywhere in the known universe. That is how scientists and engineers can build planes and transportation networks across the globe, and spaceships that fly to the moon and back again, precisely because the laws of physics *are* the same for all observers and work the same everywhere and anywhere we may go.

So by the time of Newton, scientific work was beginning to pay off in a big way and this scientific and technological pay off that was about to begin had some important features relevant to our discussion.

1. The earth was no longer the center of the universe. Man no longer held a special place as honorary observer of life.

2. Natural motion was seen as straight-line motion at a constant speed.

3. Motion through space was now seen as relative. That is, there was no absolute meaning to a declaration of motion or rest without reference to something else.

4. The laws governing this motion were the same for everyone, *all* observers in *any* frame of reference in uniform motion.

To put it more simply perhaps, if you drop a ball on the ground, it will bounce back up into your hand. If you drop it on the deck of an airplane flying along at a steady speed, it will do the same thing. And you'll get the same result on another planet, albeit at a different velocity perhaps. Yet the ball will react according to Newton's laws of gravity everywhere in the known universe equally well for all observers in uniform motion. All observers everywhere have a right to say that their observations, their measurements, are valid and conform to the known laws of physics. This is what came to be accepted as the classical laws of mechanics, or motion of objects.

(Note: Don't be confused thinking that these laws are only relevant for observers in uniform motion. It's just that until

1915 when Einstein published his General Theory of Relativity, which expanded his initial Special Theory of Relativity of 1905 to include accelerated motion, the topic was too difficult to tackle. But his General Theory of Relativity ultimately removes the restriction on uniform motion, finally granting equal status to all observers regardless of their states of motion.)

The Good, the Bad and the Ugly

The good news about all this was that, by the time of Newton, humankind was beginning to get a handle on how things worked. He was beginning to appreciate what has become known as the Clockwork Universe, a universe in which, knowing the natural laws, a scientist could determine how things worked. Indeed, this worldview came to be known as Determinism. Imagine it. If you knew that natural motion was straight-line motion at a constant speed, and your understanding of the laws of gravity could show you how and in what way objects would react to those forces, you could eventually determine virtually anything. Perfect knowledge was indeed a possibility! The universe was like a giant billiard table. All you needed to know was the current position and momenta (i.e., direction and velocity) of all objects on it, and your understanding of gravitational effects would tell you how those objects would interact with each other and where they'd end up at any point in space and time. If we could just get the current positions and momenta of all objects in the universe into some grand computer, we could predict precisely what would happen in the future, either to an apple on a tree, or a planet in the heavens. If they can map all the DNA in the human body, why couldn't they map the universe?

The bad news was that some of these findings were beginning to counter some long held beliefs, especially in the West. The Copernican Revolution, aided by proof from Galileo, forced a very important shift in Western Man's idea of his place in the cosmos. If Earth was no longer at the center of the cosmos, what did that say about Man's place in the eyes of God? In areas controlled by the Catholic Church by the time of the Inquisition, there was a very real fear of introducing these unarguable findings of science. Galileo, you might say, got off lightly, but there were others who were burned at the stake for such heresy.

That's the ugly part. For in it we can view an essential ingredient of man's self-induced suffering that I've touched upon earlier. As an old cowboy cigarette commercial proclaimed that we'd "rather fight than switch". The human animal has evolved to live largely by the stories we use to justify ourselves and our ways. Without these stories we feel lost and alone, not knowing who we are or what to do. The refutation of our stories can cause so much stress and grief that we'll do anything to uphold them, from denying all evidence to the contrary on the one hand, to killing its messengers on the other.

It's a sad but inescapable fact that the most dangerous thing in human history has often been…the truth.

Chapter Four

THE ABSOLUTE LIGHT
The Importance of Einstein

In Physics

I clearly remember that in my childhood there came a time when I wondered if other people saw things the same way I did. I wondered if it was even possible to find out. If a friend and I were looking at someone's face, for example, how could we ever know if we saw it the same way? I wondered if what I saw would seem like a monster to him, and what he saw might seem like a monster to me if we could somehow trade each other's brains. We would of course both nod our heads in agreement if shown a picture of this person's face, but this would not settle the issue since the picture, apparently, was objective and the subjective experience would remain impossible to relate.

Much of human life depends on social agreement. Our laws and norms are in essence an agreement upon our perception. We must first come to some agreement on what is real and then agree on how we want to deal with it.

Science is even more bound by this dictate. Every theory must be proven in the laboratory and the findings verified by other scientists across the globe. Only then is it considered true, or factual, and can then be used to further knowledge and technology in the service of humankind. As we saw in the previous chapter, Galileo proved that Copernicus was correct and eventually this proof was accepted around the world. This Copernican Principle, that the earth holds no central or special place in the cosmos, was expanded by the Principle of Galilean Relativity which insists that the laws of motion are valid for *all* observers in uniform motion. There is no special place of observation that is *truer* than any other place. The whole of modern scientific understanding is built upon these principles.

Yet, even so, the study of electromagnetism provided a real challenge for physicists in the 19th century. Light itself was found to be a type of electromagnetic wave that traveled through space at 186,000 miles per second, or about 670,000,000 miles per hour. In physics, this is known as *speed C*. But precisely because of the accepted understanding of the relativity of motion that we touched on in the last chapter, the obvious question had to be asked, "Light travels at that speed C relative to what?"

This was a real stumper. Physicists could find nothing that light traveled at speed C relative to. Their technology was sophisticated enough to tell them that light didn't necessarily travel at speed C relative to its source. And the concept of something called ether that permeated space through which light could be propagated, like waves through the ocean, was ruled out by the famous Michelson-Morley experiment in 1887. A similar problem was that physicists measuring the speed of light were all getting the same answer, no matter what their frames of reference were. You might think, "So what? You already said the laws of physics were valid for all observers in uniform motion in any frame of reference." Yes, but according to classical physics and Newton's laws of motion, precisely because the laws of physics are valid for all observers, their measurements should indeed be different given differing frames of reference.

Physicists would indeed expect to measure the velocity of light and get different answers if they were moving relative to that source of light, either toward it or away from it, the way that classical Newtonian physics would insist upon. If he were standing still, relative to the light source, he might expect to measure the speed of light at 186,000 mps, or 670,000,000 mph. But if he were moving towards it at 500 mph, let's say, he would expect to see that the two speeds were now adding up to 670,000,500 mph. He would expect to see the speed of light added to his own speed of 500 mph on his measuring instrument. Likewise, if he were flying away from the light source at 500 mph, he would expect to see 669,999,500 mph, or the speed of light minus his own speed away from the source.

But the physicists of the late 19th century were not getting the expected answer at all. All observers were measuring the speed of light at precisely speed C, no matter what their frames of reference or states of motion were relative to the source of light. Think carefully about their dilemma for a moment. A long line of distinguished scientists culminating with Galileo and Newton went to a lot of trouble, including risking and losing their very lives, to ultimately present mankind with the Principle of Galilean Relativity and Newton's laws of motion. Were we so soon to be forced to abandon those understandings which provided solid answers to a myriad of questions simply because we couldn't find a frame of reference for light? Were the laws of physics so limited that they couldn't include electromagnetism in their scope? Was there perhaps something wrong with their measurements? Remember, they're thought of as laws simply because they're supposed to work everywhere in the known universe.

Albert Einstein puzzled over this problem for ten years before he came up with the solution to this dilemma. And it was about time! Basically, what Einstein did was merely restate the Principle of Galilean Relativity and apply it to electromagnetism and the study of light. This may sound simple, but its implications were profound. Although everyone knew that motion through space was a relative concept, they did not know that time was likewise relative. Newton's Clockwork Universe was assumed to have an absolute timepiece somewhere, probably in God's very hand, which ticked along at the same pace for all observers. Time was thought of as absolute. But in 1905, Einstein, a lowly Swiss patent clerk, published a paper entitled, "On the Electrodynamics of Moving Bodies," which came to be known as the Theory of Special Relativity. It's 'special' because it involved only observers in uniform motion, obviously a special condition. Yet it demolished the classically held view of time itself.

His theory states, quite boldly, that the combined speed of an object's motion through space *and its motion through time* is always precisely equal to the speed of light. This means that the three dimensions of space (length, width and height) and the one dimension of time would now have to be viewed as an indissoluble continuum of space-time, the fabric of the universe. The faster an object moves through space, the slower it moves through time. Just as space and motion were understood in absolute terms before Copernicus and Galileo, now time also would have to relinquish its claim to any absolute status.

Einstein's genius was to merely restate the Principle of Galilean Relativity and apply it to the study of light. There was nothing wrong with anyone's measurements. They were indeed all correct. And remember the original question? Light travels at speed C relative to what? Einstein's answer was simple: relative to *all* observers in any frame of reference in uniform motion. And why? Precisely because the *speed* of light *is absolute.* The absolute nature of the speed of light makes individual measurements of space and time relative.

The most famous example of this, and the one which highlights the profound shock of this discovery, is the time traveling twins thought experiment. If my twin brother and I were both 20 years old and he decided to travel to a star that was 10 light-years away by my measurement, and his space ship took him at 0.8 C (or eight-tenths the speed of light), it would take him 25 years to make the round trip. Again, remember that this is my measurement of his trip here on Earth. In his reference frame, the spaceship, traveling at that speed he would measure the trip as taking only 15 years. Both our measurements are correct, and he indeed would come back 10 years younger than I, although he and I were the same age when he left. The very speed at which he traveled would cause the dilation of time, or the stretching and slowing of the processes of his body and spaceship as he journeyed. Because both of our measurements are correct, yet different, there can be no absolute or objective reality to any particular measurement. Far from being a fixed timepiece that ticks along at the same pace for everyone, time is more like a river that flows and bends in union with the space to which it is inextricably linked.

Look at it this way: what does it take to measure the speed of light?

Basically it takes something like a yardstick and a stopwatch. So if your yardstick is 186,000 miles long and you click your stopwatch when the light hits one end and click it again when light hits the other end, you'll see that one second has elapsed. But of course this is not practical; no one has such an immense yardstick. But you get the idea. We can have a much smaller yardstick if our stopwatch is more precise and we'll still be able to measure the speed of light precisely. But if you're moving toward the source of light, or away from it, when you measure it, that motion itself actually shortens the yardstick and slows the time on your stopwatch, and in precise proportion, because the combination of an object's motion through space plus its motion through time is always precisely equal to the speed of light. Motion of an object through space, like you or the yardstick, contracts the object in the direction of travel and the process of time dilates, or slows down, relative to that same object if it were stationary. That's why all physicists would measure the speed of light in different frames of reference yet get the same answer; both the yardstick and the stopwatch are proportionately affected by that movement. Only the study of light and the realization of the absolute nature of its speed finally taught man about the true nature of the relative constructs of space and time. Because the speed of light is absolute, measurements of velocities, distances and elapsed time are relative.

As I pointed out in the last chapter, Einstein's initial revelation about the relative nature of space and time arose from his Theory of Special Relativity in 1905 that was limited to uniform motion. But he was able to expand that understanding ultimately to include accelerated motion as well with his General Theory of Relativity in 1915, ultimately erasing any limitation on what has become known simply as The Theory of Relativity.

There are actually those who criticize this scientific work, and the work of others, as mere theories. But Einstein's Relativity is not some wild idea he ran up the flagpole to see who'd salute. It's been tested and verified countless times and is used everywhere in daily life today. Television sets must take time dilation into account or pictures would be blurry. GPS satellites must also take into account relativistic effects on time experienced on orbiting satellites; if not, the coordinates received by pilots in their cockpits would be off by a good part of a mile. In this case, if relativity were not understood and incorporated into the technology, disaster would result.

In Zen
During Zen Buddhist services in our lineage, there is a dedication that reads:

The absolute light, luminous throughout the whole universe; unfathomable excellence penetrating everywhere....

This is my favorite phrase in all of Zen Buddhist liturgy. It expresses the essence of Buddhist enlightenment, the realization of the absolute nature of existence.

Zen emphasizes two aspects of reality, the Absolute and the Relative. Appreciating the Absolute is essential in being able to rest comfortably in the Relative nature of our lives. The opposites of self and other, night and day, good and bad, right and wrong, man and woman…these opposites can, and will, cause endless friction if we cannot understand that their Absolute essential nature is one and the same.

The metaphor of Light is often used in Zen literature to describe this Absolute nature. As I mentioned in Chapter One, Shaku Soen Roshi explained the experience of enlightenment as, "…seeing the lamp of eternity shining through the mists of transiency." A famous Zen text, used by all students in our lineage is entitled, *The Record of Transmitting the Light*. It describes the enlightenment of all the Zen ancestors from Shakyamuni Buddha up to the Japanese Master Koun Ejo of the 13th century. The whole idea of passing on the critical teaching of Zen was actually thought of as a transmission of Light, the wisdom of the Buddha.

Within one of the cases of the text, the author Master Keizan, who was actually Master Koun Ejo's dharma grandson, describes Buddha, Mind or our True Nature as, "…nothing but bright light existing brilliantly." He advises his monks to, "…become like the great ocean without waves. Then you will have some experience of it."

This analogy of the ocean and its waves is often used, not only in Zen, but in many mystical traditions. It's as if our normal consciousness sees nothing but the waves and is unable to appreciate the ocean that connects and gives life to them all.

The bedrock of all Buddhist teaching is enlightenment, or a deep realization of the Absolute. It is here that the practitioner finally sees the ocean itself, or, to put it more precisely, realizes himself or herself as that ocean, or that light which penetrates everywhere. There is nothing independent or separate about the waves. They are merely force fields moving through the ocean. It is the ocean that connects, sustains and gives life equally to all of them. It is the Light that breathes through absolutely *all* of existence. Or, to be more precise, it is the Light which breathes *as* all of existence. Everything we are, everything we do and everything we experience is nothing but that Light.

And in Zen, as in physics, it is the Absolute nature of our True Selves that makes all individual perception and understanding of life relative. That is, everything one can see, hear, smell, taste, touch, feel and know about life is merely another wave on that ocean. In that sense it is true, valid and real, yet particular to that person's genetic heritage and mental condition. Our perceptions may and indeed often must be different from those of others, precisely because their perspectives are different. Their particular motion through the space and time of their lives inescapably equates to a different perception.

In one interpretation of relativistic physics, even our notions of past, present and future cannot be considered as real, because special relativity shows, for example, that from someone's particular perspective (far out in space), my past may not yet have happened. And from some other, equally valid perspective, my future is already finished. There is no objective (or absolute) reality ascribed to any particular measurement of space and time. The only thing that is real is the totality of space-time.

Of course, this is a vague concept. How can one grasp something so vast as space-time? In Zen, how can one grasp the Absolute? Or to put it in Christian terms, how can one grasp the very nature of God? Of course the answer is…we can't! It's impossible to intellectually grasp the vastness of our True Nature. But the good news is that humans are comprised of much more than their intellects. We all possess what is called in Buddhism, a third eye, that can realize this Absolute non-intellectually, and this realization then enlightens the mind to its True Nature. No longer lost and wandering in the stormy seas of the relative alone, the mind now rests comfortably in its absolute source, at peace with its own waves, or the fleeting manifestations that comprise what we know of and call, for want of a better term, the real world.

The Integration
Zen and other mystical traditions have throughout history challenged so-called common sense views of the world as being limited in understanding and often harmful in application. Einstein's Theories of Relativity not only had the practical applications we have just seen, and many more, they revolutionized some basic understandings of mankind.

The most basic teaching of Zen is that, essentially, we are nothing but Emptiness itself, and the Absolute nature of this Light is the essential nature of all life everywhere. As Christians would say, "We are all God's children." The practical extension of this philosophy is the understanding that we are, as we say in Zen, whole and complete just as we are. And the important point is, so is everyone else.

In physics, the speed of light, speed C, was now seen as the one absolute arbiter of the measurements of space and time. Because the speed of light was measured the same by all observers, its absolute nature meant that all individual measurements of velocities, distances and elapsed times by individual observers were valid, yet relative. If two distinct measurements are both correct, yet different, there can be no objective reality to them. They can and indeed must be different if our frames of reference are different.

Remember Einstein's answer to the dilemma of why all physicists were getting the same value for the speed of light? It was, simply, because the laws of physics are valid for *all* observers in uniform motion. Remember it was only the study of light that first presented this problem to physicists. Newton's classical physics understood that different frames of reference would yield understandably different answers. Different frames of reference logically yield different answers. And though the study of light threw a curveball at physicists for a long time, eventually Einstein solved the puzzle by emphatically restating what they already knew: that the laws of physics were indeed true for all observers. Yet the study of light showed that, because its speed is absolute, individual measurements of both space and time are relative to the observer. Likewise, the philosophy of Zen would answer the question of why we as human beings can live on this planet, presumably living the same life at the same time yet see the world in completely different ways, in exactly the same manner. Our individual perceptions can be very different, one from the other, and indeed should logically be so if our frames of reference are different. This is a classical view, similar to the view of physicists before Einstein after Galilean Relativity was accepted as fact. Yet in physics, one measurement, i.e., the speed of light, is the same regardless of the observer's frame of reference. Therefore, it is absolute. In Zen, it is precisely because we are all essentially the Absolute Light itself, the wisdom of the unfolding universe, that everyone's individual experiences and perceptions are true and valid even though they may differ in comparison. It was Einstein's restatement of the principle of Galilean Relativity that expanded the relativistic approach from space alone to finally include time, thereby creating a universe composed of a fabric of space-time whose totality represented a unity of four dimensions that could not be grasped but whose individual aspects could be relativistically measured. The tradition of Zen has always taught that our True Nature, the Light of Emptiness, is ungraspable yet manifests constantly as the life we all live, no matter how, no matter where, even though comparisons of seemingly similar perceptions and experiences may differ.

Imagine the consternation that that understanding, in Zen and in physics, caused in various circles. Since man first began serious consideration of something called truth, he became very serious about honest observation of the natural world to determine what objective reality might be. And this honest observation and the wonderful knowledge derived from it was the main reason for the advancement of not only scientific knowledge but human understanding as a whole.

All fields of human endeavor, from philosophy to religion, from science to politics, even to military tactics, held, at least as an underlying assumption, that truth is indeed something that could be found, understood and relayed to others, and that, as a society, any society, we could learn the nature of reality and apply our understanding effectively and efficiently in our lives. And where knowledge failed us, religion could apply a belief structure that explained things that science could not study, thereby calming the agitation of a spiritually inquisitive mind, that, left untended, might cause an individual or a society divisive harm.

Now along comes Einstein, who boldly claims that, ultimately, measurements of space and time are relative because the speed of light is absolute. Zen emphatically claims that the essential nature of life is Emptiness, and the Absolute nature of this reality permeates all of existence. Because of this truth, everything, without exception, is perfect, whole and complete as it is, even though comparison would make individual entities and perceptions seem superficially at odds. Think for a moment of the meaning of this. What we know of life, and how we use that knowledge to direct our actions, arises from our perceptions. And these perceptions are in a very real sense a measurement of matter and energy moving through space-time. Can you think of one thing that is not woven from the matter and energy that emerges through and is inextricably framed in the canvas of space and time? This book in your hands, the glasses on your face, the thoughts in your head…everything we are is nothing but a child of space and time, i.e., space-time. The matter and energy of the cosmos that coalesces and finds its life in any corner of space flowing through time is nothing other than you, here, reading this book. And now Einstein says that because light is an absolute measurement, measurements we previously thought of as true for all observers, now had to be accepted as merely relative to their particular frames of reference. Einstein's absolute light does not make individual measurements incorrect. Indeed, it makes them perfectly true, yet relative to that particular observer's movement through space and time.

Likewise, Zen insists that our individual perceptions are brilliant illusions: vital, clear and true, yet ephemeral and elusive, unfixed and totally dependent upon a variety of forces which can neither be fully understood nor grasped, and are dependent on the individual's own particular life circumstances. They are relative.

How can we ever understand the truth, or reality, if our measurements, our perceptions, are merely relative? How can I ever take a stand for the truth or what's right if those whose measurements and perceptions that differ from mine have equally valid positions?

A philosopher/physicist could enter at this point with a sincere objection. He or she might argue that the measurements of which I speak are seen in extreme cases only. These measurements of special relativity which differ with different observers is something only noticeable at speeds approaching the speed of light, which is a whole lot faster than anyone has ever gone. He or she would argue that I'm using an extreme example to embark on a relativistic approach to philosophy and religion. Isn't this absurd? Physicists have measured the differences in elapsed time in two frames of reference at normal speeds. They once took an atomic clock on an airplane around the earth and compared it to a similar clock that stayed on the ground. And indeed, as expected, the flying clock had a lesser elapsed time. But by how much? A whopping 300 nanoseconds less. That's 300 billionths of a second less. Are you going to use that to argue we should build a bonfire and burn the Bible, the Torah, the Koran and the Bhagavad-Gita? (Maybe not, but there are a few talk shows I'd like you to consider.)

And one of these concerned physicists was Einstein himself. He said, "I never understood why the theory of relativity with its concepts and problems so far removed from practical life should for so long have met with a lively, or indeed passionate, resonance among broad circles of the public."

With all due respect to Einstein, my point is this: just because it's extremely subtle doesn't mean it's not true. Just because it's only noticeable with highly refined scientific instruments doesn't mean it's not a fact we can ignore except to our own detriment. Mystics and Zen Masters throughout history have gone through the severest of disciplines to break through the veil of the dualistic intellect, or the common sense view of reality that has been the legacy of the human mind. They were convinced that it was limited and ultimately conducive to suffering. It was a truth not easily seen, yet vital to an enlightened appreciation of existence. The study of light and the realization of Emptiness indeed does require the highly sophisticated instruments of science and the deeper levels of the human mind. They reveal a truth not easily accepted nor appreciated by many people. But beyond a shadow of a doubt, humanity suffers not only from the natural calamities of life but also by its inability to appreciate the subtleties of a reality that may be difficult to grasp.

Our common sense view of the world is often built around the severe limitations of a rational mind that, until the last hundred years, has been hampered by the lack of any real scientific understanding of life. Humankind's intense need to know has therefore been condemned to create mythologies about how the world must work from often limited understanding of facts. Our philosophies and religions have largely been dictated by the dualistic intellect, unable and afraid to go beyond its natural limitations.

Think about it for a moment. Your eyes and ears can see and hear only certain frequencies. Your taste buds and senses of smell and touch are dictated by the slow yet inevitably divergent process of evolution, different in preference and sensitivity from other species. Every color you see, every sound you hear, every taste you have, is experienced by you in a particular way *not* because that's the way *it is*, but only as by-product of a filtering process that your evolving biology dictates.

And your mind, which is itself evolving, is there trying to make sense of it all, cataloguing and filing away information at breakneck speed, yet only able to process the limited data it receives from the natural world which is filtered and contorted by the limitations of the senses it's attached to. By the time a human child is several months old, its brain has already trained itself to exclude a large percentage of the sensory data that surrounds it. If it didn't, its circuit breakers would pop; there's just too much data in the natural world for any one being to take in. And different species have different abilities to extract data from the natural world according to their own particular paths of evolution. A dog hears different frequencies than we do and sees different colors. A chameleon's eyes rotate on two different axes with independently moving eyeballs. What would it see if it were in your room right now? What philosophy would the chameleon create to understand that room? And what religion would it create to explain that room and defend at all costs as the one true faith?

We all unconsciously believe our perception is infallible, that it sees reality. But it is merely an interpretation, an experience drawn from a simultaneous coalescing of only a limited amount of data from a vast field of energy. In our case as humans on this planet, our perception is imprisoned not only by the constraints of evolution, but also by our inability to move at high speeds, and the inability to understand how nature functions at miniscule subatomic levels.

Religion provides mankind with a sense of his place in the grand order of things, and hopefully with a true sense of peace and comfort in the cosmos when confronted by the awful chasm of the unknown. But if it is only a belief system bolstered by the delusion of a dualistic intellect, problems can arise because we don't recognize that it is the intellect itself that creates the chasm. The ossification that the intellect imprints on our perception creates the deep-seated dualism of self and other, good and bad, right and wrong, God and man. This unconscious tyranny of the evolved intellect creates the chasm that it then takes for a problem it must resolve. Religions, gurus, Zen Masters, yoga teachers, self-help books and talk radio - everywhere we seek someone to explain the truth of existence to us because we can't seem to appreciate that in the final analysis, we are that reality. It would be funny if the results were not so often tragic.

I like to study my cat. I find her to be an enlightened being. She eats when she's hungry and she sleeps when she's tired. I've tried to teach her about the deep truths of life, but she won't listen. I've tried to get her to sit next to me and pray, or chant the sutras, or meditate, but she refuses to do so. She merely ambles outside to find a warm place to sit in the sun, or a mouse to chase, or a comfortable place to take a fine nap. She can't be seduced by anything I might try to tell her. She lives totally from her own being. I'm not disgusted. Just envious.

Buddhism's biggest claim is that it has something valuable to say about suffering. And that claim is that a large part of our suffering is self-induced, not through any masochistic dysfunction, but merely because we are blinded by the delusion of a limited and habituated perception of the world thought to be the whole truth. And seeing through these cells of our own construction is vital to releasing the terrible shackles of our inheritance.

Chapter Five

NO SUCH THING AS A SMALL THING
The Importance of Quantum Mechanics

In Buddhism

Have you ever touched a spider's web and noticed how just the slightest tap at any point on the web vibrates the whole system?

Many years ago, Maezumi Roshi, one of the pioneers of Zen in the West, was holding a Zen retreat (sesshin) at a private home in Mexico. Even though it was in someone's house, the members still conducted the retreat with some of the traditional ritual as would be used in a monastery or Zen Center. There was chanting, black-robed monks and students doing walking meditation in the garden, and other activities foreign to the neighborhood. At some point during the week, a neighbor's dog happened to dash across the street and was hit by an automobile and killed. Maezumi Roshi announced that they would perform a memorial service for the neighbor's dog, insisting that their retreat was a causal factor in the dog's death. He was challenged on this point by some students who argued that they'd barely noticed the dog next door and no one had even approached or spoken to it. Roshi persisted by arguing that their retreat had upset the dog in some subtle way and was indeed a factor in making the dog anxious enough to do something that he normally wouldn't do, such as dash blindly across a street near which he'd lived safely for years. When Roshi was asked how such a small thing as their silent presence next door could cause such a catastrophe, he replied, "There's no such thing as a small thing."

One of the critical aspects of the Buddhist enlightenment discussed earlier was the realization of the relative nature of perception. In short, we come to see our lives as brilliant illusions, ephemeral yet energetic, powerful yet elusive. This is an inescapable fact of the Light of Emptiness. Like physical light itself, our lives shine everywhere with the energy of the universe, brilliant yet impossible to grasp. And most importantly, not only our lives but the life of everyone and everything is likewise blessed.

But there is another important aspect to this realization, and it is often called Oneness, Interbeing or the Interconnectedness of all life. Generally speaking, human consciousness automatically and habitually creates a dualistic framework of perception and usually sees and experiences a separation of oneself from the rest of existence. Buddhist philosophy identifies this limited framework, and the various skillful means of its practice aim at freeing the student from these confines and opening him or her to the broader experience of spaciousness and unity of their True Nature.

Human societies, especially in the West, have accepted the ingrained dualistic framework so thoroughly that even challenging its cultural offspring has seemed foolish at best, and blasphemous at worst. We seem to accept without question such spiritual separations as God and man and right and wrong, and such spatial separations as here and there. And we have no doubts about the usual temporal separations of past and future.

But why do we take these relative constructs and make them absolute? Why do we ascribe to them an unquestioned validity that is always true to a sane person, and only doubtful to a madman? Jesus said, "Before Abraham came to be, I AM." And Buddha, upon his enlightenment said, "Below the heavens, above the earth, I alone AM." The expression of Jesus represents a challenge to the temporal limitations we've inherited, while Buddha's expression challenges our spatial limitations. Put them together and you have an expression of a profound realization of Oneness that transcends our *normal* perceptions of both space and time. Actually this realization that shatters the barriers of an imprisoned dualistic consciousness does not *transcend* our habitual dualisms so much as it *encompasses* them into an inclusive framework where *past* and *future,* and *here* and *there,* are enfolded into NOW and HERE!

Once, during the noon meal at a formal retreat at the Zen Center of Los Angeles, I was looking in my bowl at some cooked carrots and I began to stare at them in an unusual way. Somehow my vision had expanded to see the vast interconnected history of myself and what I was about to eat. I could sense the history of matter and energy, of life, that had moved inexorably through an eternity of time and through a variety of forms - through soil, light, and heat to become today's carrots; through genes, blood and bones to become today's cooks; and through other elements to become the knives, bowls and chopsticks that brought the food in that shining, timeless moment, to me. I almost couldn't eat it. It was too beautiful to touch.

There is a Zen phrase, emphatically stated by many masters, which says simply, "JUST THIS!" But far from a phrase denoting an ignorance of or a rejection of anything not immediately available to our perception, it is an all-encompassing expression of the vast reality of space and time that is now appreciated as being totally enfolded perfectly into whatever lies before the Mind's Eye. For HERE and NOW is really nothing less than a manifestation of eternity.

In Physics

There is in the world of physics a reality that is wonderfully analogous to this idea of Oneness and Unity. In the sometimes dry jargon of physics it's called both *nonlocality* and *entanglement*. As in our previous discussion of Einstein's Relativity, it all began with the modern study of light.

Conducting his experiments in the early part of the 19th century, British scientist Thomas Young concluded that light functioned as a continuous wave of energy. He is important to remember because the experiment he used to prove this would maintain its importance well into the quantum age as the first experiment to signify the dilemma and wonder of quantum mechanics. It remains famous today as the *split-screen experiment*. Thomas Young used it to show that the nature of light was a wave. Basically, with a light source shining through two slits in a barrier, the resulting interference pattern displayed on a screen behind the barrier demonstrated that light functioned as a wave, much the same way as ocean waves passing through two narrow openings in a harbor jetty will show a similar interference pattern inside the harbor.

But within a hundred years of Thomas Young's certainty, there arose several problems with the wave description of light. Basically, this classical description failed to hold up under new experiments in physics. Most notably, Einstein showed that a description of light as a particle, rather than a wave, best described the photoelectric effect. This phenomenon is seen experimentally where electrons are ejected from a metal surface immediately upon being hit by a photon of light, like a cue ball knocking a billiard ball off a pool table. Only the description of light as a particle, rather than a wave, satisfactorily explained this experiment at that time.

So, just to be sure, scientists decided to pull Thomas Young's split-screen experiment out of the proverbial closet and check it again. His experiment was conducted many times throughout the many laboratories of physics. They found that, like Thomas Young, with both slits in the barrier open, a wave interference pattern was produced but if they closed one of the slits, light behaved like a beam of particles. How could light act one way under one experiment and another way under a different experiment? Simply put, how did light know that one of the slits was closed? They even did the experiment where only one photon of light (Einstein's particle of light) at a time was emitted at a barrier with two slits open. Yet a wavelike interference pattern was created even then. How could one particle, one photon, interfere with itself?

Physicists eventually accepted that light had a dual nature, both wave and particle. How it appeared depended on the experiment that was used to test it. And not only that, but it was later shown that not just mass-less particles like photons of light, but actual matter itself, like electrons (and by inference even macroscopic objects like you and me) were shown to have wave properties, as well. It is believed that all matter has wave characteristics associated with it.

We know that everyday matter, from water to rocks to you and me, is made up of molecules and those molecules are made up of atoms. Atoms themselves are formed by a nucleus consisting of protons and neutrons, with electrons in orbit around that nucleus. But we can't actually consider these *particles* like little BBs, or little balls in motion, because of the wave/particle duality previously mentioned. Whether these electrons, protons and neutrons are *particles* of matter or *waves* of energy depends upon the way we look at them, the experiment we set up to detect them.

Imagine for a moment tossing an electron into a box. Since it is both wave and particle, if we partition the box into two, where exactly is the particle? A continuous wave can spread throughout the box, whereas a particle must have a definite position. Only a particular experiment will tell us where the particle is located which is analogous to opening the box and looking inside the two partitions. But where is the particle *before* we open the box and look? That is, in which partition does it reside? Does it indeed *have* any particular position without us detecting it?

In this subatomic realm, where matter and energy, where life itself to our human view, can't seem to make up its mind as to what exactly it is, very strange behaviors take place. As in the split-screen experiment mentioned earlier where only one photon of light at a time was emitted at the barrier yet somehow still created a wave interference pattern on the screen behind, somehow this one photon was in two places at once, going through both barriers and interfering with itself on the other side. Yet if we try to detect that one photon, or even an electron in a box, and nail it down to a specific location, we can do so, but in so doing we lose its wavelike nature. The wave function is said to *collapse* at that moment. It is this wave function that allows a phenomenon called *quantum tunneling*, where a particle that is seemingly locked in a barrier can instantly appear outside that barrier, like a prisoner in a cell suddenly appearing outside of that cell without ever being seen to go through a door or break through the wall. This *quantum tunneling* is partially responsible for nuclear processes inside our sun that provide the light and heat necessary for our survival.

The reason that we don't see strange quantum behaviors in our macroscopic world is that these behaviors are only noticeable in environments where the wavelength of the associated particle is comparable to the size of the environment it's operating in. For example, the wavelength of an electron is comparable to the size of the atom, and bizarre behaviors like quantum tunneling and the aforementioned particle/wave dualities are easily noticed. An example in our larger world is your television set. Did you ever wonder why, when you leave the room with the TV still on, you can still hear it, but not see it? Sound waves are large and comparable to the size of the openings in doorways and windows, whereas light waves are small in comparison with that environment. Therefore, the sound acts like waves bending and flowing through the house while the light shines straight ahead in a beam of particles. If light waves were similar in size to sound waves we could go anywhere in the house and still watch television, but with similar distortion in sound and picture.

Perceiver and Perceived are One
It is important to clearly understand the problem presented here. Buddhism has always addressed the phenomena of perception by noting that perceiver and perceived are One and ultimately cannot be functionally separated, while classical Western thought has assumed that perceiver and perceived are ultimately separate and can be studied as such. You'll recall from Chapter One that Sir Isaac Newton's classical physics saw the world in deterministic ways. That is, the observer could study and *determine* what nature *really was* precisely because observer and observed, scientist and nature, were ultimately separate and different entities, with definite and discernible attributes. Therefore the *state* of nature could clearly be studied, observed, understood and catalogued for future reference. Buddhism has never denied that such study is proper and beneficial; it only insists that it is a partial view and, when taken as the only view, can cause problems.

The split-screen experiment was the first scientific inkling in Western classical physics that perhaps *determinism* was not the whole story. Here was an experiment that defied a deterministic approach. The split-screen experiment shows us that *what* we see depends on *how* we look, and *how* we look clearly effects *what* we see.

Buddhism has always addressed observation from a similar angle. In the earliest Zen texts found that date from the first part of the Tang dynasty in China (618-907 CE), there is a discussion of this dynamic. It goes something like this: imagine the dynamic of sight for a moment, or, in Buddhism, *eye-consciousness*. For *eye-consciousness* to exist, there must be, at the very least, an object to see, a seer of that object and a mind to process the seeing. But if we try to nail down where exactly this *seeing*, this *eye-consciousness* comes from, we can easily get lost. Blind people have minds, but they cannot see. Dead people have eyes, but they cannot see, either. Objects are inert and cannot produce *eye-consciousness* by themselves. None of these three essentials can act alone to produce sight. It takes a dynamic interplay of all three to produce something we call *sight*. Likewise, all the consciousness we have of life itself functions in a similar way. Whatever we may call *consciousness* is, in fact, an interplay of forces that cannot be realistically separated in Buddhist understanding. They can only be separated in the mythology of the stories we tell about life, and never in the actual dynamic functioning of existence.

Someone may argue in the following vein: "Nonsense! We use deterministic laws of science everyday. And perfectly well, mind you. You're a pilot. You should know that. You use Newton's laws of motion every time you fly from L.A. to New York and they give you very exact knowledge about the flying time, don't they?"

I would respond this way: Newton's laws of motion do give me very exact information of my projected flight time…ON PAPER! But reality doesn't live on paper. The map is not the territory. In truth, a variety of forces, from late baggage, to higher than projected winds, from maintenance malfunctions to passenger illness often wreak havoc with projected flight times.

And you may respond that those are not problems with Newton's laws, but from other unknown factors. And I would answer that that's my point entirely. Newton's deterministic laws of motion work well in the story we've created about airline flying. But the reality of that flying encompasses a vast variety of factors and forces that function constantly in the undivided and interconnected *real* world that cannot possibly be fully known or controlled.

So, in the world of physics, it became accepted that we could not study the subatomic realm in its *essential state* without changing it in some way. The mere fact of our observation actually affected and altered whatever we were looking at. Light was seemingly coy by presenting to us different results depending on our experiments, different answers depending on our questions. Rather than accept this as an unavoidable contradiction, the physicist Neils Bohr chose to develop the concept of *complementarity*. Basically, if you're looking for wave-like behavior, you will find it. And if you're looking for particle behavior, you will find that, as well. But you'll never find both at the same time. When we're looking at the night sky, we cannot see the day, and vice versa. Even though a coin has two sides, we can only view one side at a time. This is dictated by our own perceptual limitations, and not by any contradiction on the part of nature.

You'll recall from Chapter Two that the study of physics was basically a study of motion, observing and understanding the position and momentum of objects in the universe. As we saw earlier in this chapter with the *electron in a box* thought experiment, this need to understand exact position and momenta of objects becomes quite problematic in quantum mechanics. With this understanding, physicist Werner

Heisenberg, working in the 1920s, showed us that we could never measure exactly *both* the position *and* momentum of a particle. This became known as the Heisenberg Uncertainty Principle. The more accurately we could determine one facet, such as position, the less accurately we could measure the other facet, such as momentum, and vice versa. The observer and his observed particle were linked so intimately in this dance of observation that getting very accurate information about one factor, by itself, contaminated information about the other. It is impossible to observe the quantum realm without affecting it.

Realize what a major problem this was. Classical physics relied on determining exact positions and momenta of objects, the very mechanics of life. Being able to accurately determine the future relies completely on accurate information about the present state of these factors. If at the subatomic realm this was truly not possible, then even in our macroscopic world we would be condemned to measurements whose complete accuracy would remain forever in doubt. Infinitely precise measurements would never be possible.

Neils Bohr, and others, extended Heisenberg's Uncertainty Principle philosophically into a realm known as *logical positivism*. Basically, it made no sense to talk about a particle having any specific position or momentum until it was measured. In other words, if our observations indeed *constructed* the aspects, affected them to be in a certain way, then why should we assume that these particles even had any of these aspects outside of our observations of them? In essence, it is our *observation* that *creates* the reality, a reality that doesn't necessarily exist beforehand. This view of logical positivism ran directly counter to the determinism of classical physics, and was initially rejected by many, including Einstein himself. Although Einstein accepted Heisenberg's Uncertainty Principle, for him this only meant that under the current state of technology and understanding quantum reality couldn't be accurately *determined* in a classical way. Einstein was convinced that quantum mechanics was not a complete picture of the subatomic realm. In his mind, there just had to be a classical reality even on the subatomic realm that could, in theory, be ultimately determined. His famous phrase, "God does not play dice with the universe," was his rejection of the view of Neils Bohr and others that the quantum realm did not have a definable existence absent our observations of it.

It is easy to appreciate why this debate was so crucial and so philosophically important. Remember that the quantum realm is really *our* realm, just at its smallest level. So whatever is true there must at least have some meaning, some application, for us in the larger world. If at the quantum level our observations, or the way in which we view things, indeed have a definite and measurable impact upon what we see, then what does that say about our inherited world view that there must be a reality *out there* that can be identified and agreed upon?

As in our discussion of eye-consciousness earlier, Buddhism has always considered perception, or observation, in a way similar to the approach of Neils Bohr. His approach became known as the *Copenhagen Interpretation* of quantum mechanics, taken from the city and university where he taught, and became the standard interpretation that has held sway in physics for many years, even to this day. It is by no means the only interpretation available, but is the one most useful for us as a Buddhist analogy.

I'm a golfer and I've studied the golf swing extensively. I watch the pros in slow motion and compare my horrible swing to theirs, side by side in modern video instruction. If I sense a fault in my swing, or have a revelation about swing mechanics that I feel must be true, I figure that it must at least be visible in slow motion in a professional golfer's swing. So, I'll go look for it in the videos. And you know what? I always find what I'm looking for. No matter what aspect of the swing I'm looking for, I always seem to find it. In that respect, it is my search for a particular aspect that creates it to be true. Or at least, it is that search which brings that aspect to the forefront while the other aspects, almost too numerous to mention, remain in the background, hidden for the moment from conscious appreciation.

And for quantum mechanics, the question was very similar. Does a particle indeed *have* a particular existence before we observe it? Or does our observation *create* the particular facets of its existence? This became the great scientific and philosophical debate between Albert Einstein and Neils Bohr that culminated in one of the most astonishing discoveries in the history of science.

The EPR Paradox

It's called the EPR paradox, taking its name from the physicists who proposed it, Albert Einstein, Boris Podolsky and Nathan Rosen. This was initially a thought experiment generated as an attack against Bohr and his colleagues' interpretation of quantum mechanics.

Although the original EPR paradox is quite complex, it can be simplified in the way the physicist David Bohm explained it. Subatomic particles can exhibit a characteristic called *spin*, or angular momentum, like a ball or planet spinning around any particular axis. Bohm proposed, as a thought experiment, a particle of zero spin (i.e., a particle not spinning around any axis) that was allowed to decay and split into two particles shooting off in opposite directions, each particle now *spinning* as a result of the split. The particles must have diametrically opposite spins for their sum to be zero. If we were to measure the spin of one of these new particles, let's say in the particle that flew off to the right, and found that this new particle had *up* spin, what would that say about the particle that flew off to the left? From the law of the conservation of angular momentum, the spin of both particles must still add up to zero, so the particle that flew off to the left would have to have *down* spin.

(You can imagine a small cell that, if split into two, would reconstitute itself into its original shape in the two new cells, yet the force and friction of the split could cause opposite momenta on each new shape, for example, clockwise for the one moving to the right and counter-clockwise for the one going left.)

But the EPR's paradox states that, under Bohr's Copenhagen Interpretation of quantum mechanics, it is precisely our *observation* of the spin of one particle that in fact *determines* that spin, and must thereby determine the spin of the *other* particle, as well. This is like saying if I compliment a woman on her beauty and she smiles, that her twin sister, no matter where that sister may be, even out of earshot *across the gal-*

axy, would smile instantly, as well. To EPR's proponents, this was logically absurd and a violation of the Relativity's ultimate speed limit of the speed of light. Why? Because in some way the information derived from the observation of one particle would have to be transmitted instantaneously to the other particle, no matter how far away it was, even perhaps light years away, violating that speed limit. Einstein felt that his EPR paradox was an ironclad argument against Copenhagen's standard interpretation of quantum mechanics.

But Bohr would not yield. He insisted that the Copenhagen Interpretation would still hold true. At the time Einstein and Bohr were slugging it out, this was merely a thought experiment as the technology to test it was not yet available, but gradually the technology was developed and this EPR paradox was tested, beginning in the 1970s, and many times since in ever more sophisticated experiments. And you know what? Albert Einstein was wrong!

Experiments proved that indeed the twin sister *does* smile, and physicists assume instantaneously, because she does so as fast as our atomic clocks can measure. How do we know that this defies not only Einstein's intuition (and ours), but Relativity, as well? Because in the most extensive experiment conducted in 1997, the particles tested were seven miles apart. And in the time it took the twin sister to react with a smile, light, the fastest transmitter of any kind of information we know of, could have only traveled a whopping *six inches*! Therefore it didn't matter if that twin sister was across the room, or across the universe, my compliment to one affected the other as if they were still joined at the hip. This became known as *nonlocality* because influences on one particle at a particular location can affect its *sister* particle at another location no matter where it might be. It is also known as *entanglement* because of the linked or *entangled* reactions of the particles involved.

Entanglement in physics is the perfect analogy for *Oneness* in Buddhism for it displays an arena in science that corresponds beautifully to an arena in Buddhist philosophy that has existed for over two millennia. One of the most basic tenets of Buddhism is that desire causes suffering. But this desire is in reality a futile grasping at what appears superficially to be separate aspects of our lives. It is an ignorance of the true condition of our existence which is essentially One and undivided, where grasping is unnecessary, and all the seemingly separate aspects at which we grasp are already inherently enfolded into who we truly are.

Oneness and Chaos

But is this interaction, this bizarre, "…spooky action at a distance", as Einstein called it, really seen only in the subatomic world?

A number of physicists are aware that their findings are used in modern philosophic and Buddhist arguments to talk about Oneness. Some have expressed a concern that these discussions are simplistic and exaggerated because the results of *entanglement* experiments, for example, are easily interfered with in the laboratory.

But what Buddhists call the Oneness of Existence, or the Interconnectedness of all Life, is not limited to laboratories, particle accelerators or blackboards with obscure mathematics plastered all over them. This story of Oneness does not end at the subatomic level. The interconnectedness of matter and energy, of life itself, is also readily seen in the larger world.

Modern Chaos Theory, sometimes called Complexity Theory, arose in part from the study of meteorology. With the advent of computers, scientists realized they'd now really be able to get a handle on weather prediction, a very inexact science. In 1960, a scientist named Edward Lorenz, while working on this very problem, stumbled on an amazing find. Computer simulations began to reveal that very small changes in initial conditions could lead to very large, even drastic changes in the long-term behavior of a system, like the weather. This became popularly known as the Butterfly Effect. Scientists realized that a butterfly flapping his wings in South America, for example, produces a tiny change in the atmosphere that produces another effect and then another, like dominoes falling inevitably one after the other. In a few weeks time, this snowballing effect can actually become a tornado in another part of the world, or the initial atmospheric variable could also lead to the elimination of a tornado over time, as well.

A system that was not bound by interconnectedness, in which Interbeing or Oneness was not the operative principle in the transfer of matter and energy, would not behave in this way. In a world where Dualism was the operative principle, where observer and observed were indeed separate and controllable as such, we might indeed be able to shut down cause and effect, limit and control it, and orchestrate it to our satisfaction.

There are those who might argue that we can indeed separate and control a variety of systems, and do so every day to our benefit. In fact, much of the activity of human culture is directed towards that end. From farming to behavior, from politics to war, we spend much of our time attempting to control the cause and effect of our environment, of our very lives. But our lack of understanding and appreciation of the deep and subtle interconnected nature of existence shows up in the way many of our endeavors in this arena ultimately backfire and cause unimagined grief. As we move into the 21st century, we realize that we can no longer hide from the devastating effects of pollution, short-term political *fixes*, and wars whose roots may go back to an honest desire for human progress, yet whose functioning suffers inevitably much more from poor understanding than inadequate compassion.

But the nature of our own planet's weather points to a story where the flow of causation is inevitable, precisely because Life itself *is* One and Undivided. What we see in end results large enough to be recognized by us has its birth in the subtlest of conditions, the smallest of places, yet in this most powerful and inescapable dynamic.

Air Combat

After I learned the art of air combat at Topgun, I used to teach one-versus-one dogfighting, for a time giving a lecture on that topic to various squadrons in the Pacific Fleet. Dogfighting in a modern fighter jet is probably the fastest, most powerful, most intense experience a young man can have. And, by the way, the most fun! The butterfly effect could be seen even in this arena.

In a dogfight where two jets with similar performance characteristics merge at a given altitude and given speed to begin their fight, the only variable is the pilot. Therefore, many consider one-versus-one dogfighting the best developer of overall pilot skill. When two jets meet head on, at the first *pass*, the fight often begins by the pilots turning hard back toward each other in the horizontal plane for another pass, or even two. Then often one of the pilots takes his jet up and goes vertical to redefine the fight into the vertical plane. Here the pilots often end up looping around each other in what's known as a *rolling scissors*. The pilots are always maneuvering their jets in an endless geometry of angular progression, trying desperately to get behind each other, the object being to get the nose of their jet pointing at their opponent so that they can bring their weapons to bear.

But this kind of dogfight is really a study in geometry, where the all-important factor is the individual pilot's understanding of the geometry created by the engagement, and his skill at taking advantage of his opponent's lack of that same understanding.

But after years of practice, I began to see this butterfly effect in dogfighting. That is, I noticed that very small initial differences in the geometrical angles created by the turning jets would make huge differences after only a few turns. I began to feel that I could tell the outcome of a fight often after the second pass, and certainly after the third. I noticed that good fighter pilots had either conscious or intuitive understanding of these angular differences that could be capitalized on if their opponents were undisciplined in their flying. Less skillful pilots did not see or could not appreciate the real seriousness of these small initial differences, and ultimately were defeated, not so much due to poor flying ability but to poor understanding of the geometrical environment of the dogfight, and the crucial nature of small initial conditions that can multiply quickly. Why? Because once a fight is joined, there is a spherical geometrical shape that is developed in which angular advantage or disadvantage to the pilots is created by their actions and reactions, and those very actions are dictated not only by their understanding, experience, and skill, but also critically by the interconnected nature of the geometrical shape of the fight which dictates that there is ultimately no escape, save victory, or death.

The outcome of a dogfight depends on a variety of interconnected variables, not the least of which is understanding the sensitive dependence on initial conditions and how they can multiply quickly toward defeat or victory. Systems are complex precisely because they are interconnected. What may appear in South America as an inconsequential air vibration created by a butterfly can have disastrous consequences in Bangladesh. A small angular differential between two jets in a dogfight can mean the loss of an air battle, and ultimately a geopolitical shift on our planet.

Chaos Theory deals with large complex systems while *entanglement* is a phenomenon of the subatomic world. Yet both point to interconnectedness of being that is clearly identifiable. But some might argue that the difference between these examples of interconnectedness in our visible world, and the entanglement of the subatomic world, is time. That is, whereas in the subatomic realm entanglement of particles can appear instantaneous, or interconnected in the highest sense, the butterfly effect must take time to establish itself in the macroscopic realm, therefore weakening the philosophical argument.

The Problem of Time

But is there really a time delay in our larger world? What is time, really? Einstein once said, "For we convinced physicists, the distinction between past, present and future is only an illusion, however persistent." Our usual perception of time is that it flows from past to present to future. Our human sense of time is something like watching a movie, where a frame that was lit a moment ago is now dark, and a frame to come is not yet lit by the projector. The only frame that is lit for us in the present is what we call *NOW*.

But we need to appreciate that whatever we call an experience of *now* is really just a snapshot of the past. If *now* for you is reading this book, or gazing at your garden, whatever you see and feel is already gone, because it takes *time* for the light and heat of the experience to reach your senses. If you're looking at the sun, you're seeing it as it was eight minutes ago. You're seeing the sun's past, *not* it's *now*.

Yet, just as we see the garden, the moon and the sun *out there*, just as we appreciate all of space as existing *out there*, so really does all of time. As we have already learned, space and time are just two sides of the indissoluble fabric of space-time. In physics, the whole reel of film is lit simultaneously, and it's there to be viewed by a particular observer in a particular place and state of motion in the universe. According to the equations of relativity, it is true that for a particular observer, far out in space, what I call my past has not yet happened. Yet for a different observer in a different position and state of motion, what I call my future is already finished. What we experience as a flow of time is dependent upon our particular limited observational positions, and not to any absolute truth as to the nature of time. Positions in space no more change than do moments in time. Positions in space may change, but only to *other* positions. Moments in time may change, but only to *other* moments. Each place and each moment is, in itself, a permanent fixture in the fabric of space-time. And each frame of the film of the universe remains always lit with the potential for observation.

Imagine that you and are standing together observing a solar flare through a telescope. Our experience of life, our present moment, our *NOW*, would be that experience. Yet if I were in a spaceship half way between the earth and the sun, I would be seeing that solar flare fully four minutes before you did. In that sense, I would be seeing your future, and at the moment you saw the flare here on earth, you would be viewing my past. Indeed, it is the light of Mind, of Consciousness, that illuminates the frame, even though this illumination appears to us to occur at different times.

The great Zen Master Dogen (1200-1250 CE) wrote a fascicle, or essay, on something he called *Being-Time*. His deep understanding revealed to him a mystical truth that would take another 800 years to be appreciated scientifically. He said, "Do not think that time merely flies away. Do not see flying away as the only function of time. If time merely flies away, you would be separate from time....The reason you do not clearly understand *being-time* is that you think of time as only as passing away." Einstein proved that space and time are not two different things. Likewise, Master Dogen writes that you and I are not separate from time. We are time.

In another of his brilliant works, he writes:

"Firewood turns into ash, and does not turn into firewood again. But do not suppose that the ash is after and the firewood before. We must realize that firewood is in the state of being firewood, and it has its before and after. Yet despite this past and future, its present state is *independent of them*."

Maezumi Roshi, one of my teachers, writes in an essay on Dogen's work:

"As far as our common sense goes, we think we have had a past, are having a present, and are going to have a future, that there is something that persists through all of these. But actually, each moment, each instant, is totally absolute, and past and future are included in....if you take a lighted stick of incense and rotate it in the darkness, you will see a very clear circle. Is it alive? Is it an unbroken circle? In a way, yes, and in a way, no. We think we see continuity, but it is all an illusion. It's like a movie. We see continuous motion, but actually each frame is totally independent. Our life is like that."

Remember the modern split-screen experiment where they allowed only one photon of light at a time to be emitted at a barrier with two slits open, yet still a wavelike interference pattern was produced? And the puzzling question was how could one photon interfere with itself? This seems puzzling given our normal appreciation of time but in Relativity Theory there is no time at the speed of light. It ceases to exist. So for photons of light moving at that ultimate speed there is no time at all. Only from our perspective is there a time delay between each photon, one released after the other. From the photon's perspective, it's all happening *now*. So from that point of view, is there anything puzzling about it?

Conclusion

The primary intent of Zen practice is the realization of Emptiness. It is a realization that frees us from the trap of a dualistic human intellect and evaporates the separations and boundaries of space and time. As we have seen, these separations have no absolute validity in physics and the whole history of Buddhist teaching has attempted to reveal their inadequacy.

It is remarkable that both Zen Buddhism and modern physics can speak with equal conviction of both the Relative and Absolute nature of existence. The laws of physics can show that nature is ultimately comprised of discrete and separate particles, and can also show that these same particles, when viewed from a different approach, are actually waves of continuous energy. Far from being separate, physics can show that these same particles can instantaneously affect one another no matter how far they are seemingly separated. Physics can show us how positions in space and time can be measured classically in a familiar way, and also show how the classical appreciation of space and time is merely a relative view and has no absolute basis. Likewise, the teaching of Zen does not deny the Relative, but it does insist that it is a limited approach, and that only an appreciation of the Absolute can satisfy the doubt and anxiety that a relative approach to life alone naturally produces.

Both traditions teach of the value of Relative and Absolute alike. Yet if we are locked into an approach dictated solely by the Relative, we are condemned to stumble over Absolute realities that are unavoidable. But if we can appreciate the Absolute as well, there is a real chance to loosen the knots of suffering that have bound humankind for millennia. And what this might look like, in our modern world, is the investigation we shall begin in Part II.

PART TWO

THE RELATIVE

Chapter Six

DESIRE'S CLEAR LIGHT
The Importance of Suffering

Once, long ago, I was stuck in a relationship in which I could find no joy, no peace and no escape. For reasons I hope to reveal in this chapter, I felt ensnared by a woman who played me like a yo-yo, pulling me in then throwing me out, loving me one day, then ignoring me or cheating on me the next. My desire to possess her sexually, and own her emotionally, driven in part perhaps by the fighter pilot's ego to win at all costs, did nothing but cause the most prolonged suffering of my life, a suffering intensified by her laughter at my predicament.

For a long while, my only hope was that she would end her days digging through some garbage bin somewhere. But in the end, I had to acknowledge her as one of my main teachers. Suffering is critically important for human beings because it teaches us how we often unwittingly and habitually exacerbate modest pain and create enormous suffering merely from lack of understanding.

In traditional Buddhism, desire and suffering go hand in hand. Like two sides of the same coin, flip one over and the other naturally appears. Most of us have had a variety of relationships in our lives, and usually at least one characterized by intense desire. Desire seems to offer the hope of true fulfillment and happiness on several levels, an odd mixture of biological urges and fairy tale fantasies. And at times these urges and fantasies come to fruition in a resounding, "Yes!" But, as anyone who has been there will attest, these same urges and fantasies, sooner or later, will yield an equally deafening, "Oh, NO!" The suffering of intense desire gone south has bitten everyone. The greater the desire, the more intense the suffering. It follows as surely as a bad hangover follows a night of revelry. But when I speak of desire, it is of course not limited to sexual desire, but includes all the physical, emotional, intellectual and spiritual longings we chase.

All of Buddha's teaching begins with what is known as The Four Noble Truths. The first of these truths is the teaching that life is suffering. To most people in the world today, this may seem self-evident. We often cannot get what we want, and what we get, we don't want. And even the pleasure of acquiring what we desperately pursue often seems short-lived. This desire to have the world and our lives be other than what they are causes unending tension.

There are many ways to deal with the problem of desire and suffering, and in the many sects of Buddhism you will find approaches that differ. Even in Zen Buddhism, Japanese or Korean approaches may differ from one another as American approaches may differ from theirs. These various approaches are colored by cultural differences as well as by the traits and understandings of the individual masters that teach them. I teach what I have come to find most valuable for my particular situation and the lay students I deal with.

The Dalai Lama has said that all beings want to be happy and avoid suffering. This is the natural state of sentient life, and the avoidance of suffering is readily seen in animals as well as people. It is merely a fact. Yet, on the surface, it also seems to complicate the Buddha's basic teaching. The motivation to avoid suffering and pursue happiness, can be viewed as another desire, another attachment that can only lead to further suffering. How is it ever possible to extinguish something so basic to human survival as desire?

Of course contemplative practice combined with a strict observance of the precepts of a religious life, as in the case of a monk in a monastery, can, over a long period of time, tame cravings, even desires, and provide the practitioner with peace and equanimity. At times I've heard of individuals who have tamed desire through long practice and dedication.

But when I hear this I often recall the story of the famous Roman General Scipio who defeated Hannibal at the battle of Zama in 202 BC, finally establishing Rome as the sole power in the Mediterranean. There was a famous beauty in one of the cities he conquered and he sent out an order to his men that no harm should come to her. But the lieutenant whose luck (or lack thereof) it was to enter her house found her so irresistible that he raped her anyway. For this crime, Scipio had his own officer executed, saying something to the effect that, "…there is more honor to he who has learned to tame and bridle the wild horses of lust than to he who has earned a great victory in battle."

So when I hear a story of some famous master who has, after many years of arduous practice, finally achieved a state beyond desire, I'm not sure whether he's actually tamed those wild horses or they just wandered off and died on him somewhere.

The tradition of Zen insists that, more immediately, it is an enlightened understanding that can ease the pangs of a suffering that arises more from delusion than the actual existence of natural desire.

Desire vs. Craving / Pain vs. Suffering

The Sanskrit word that we normally translate as desire is *trishna*. It is also literally translated as thirst, craving or attachment. There is an important difference here, depending on how we interpret these words. For me, desire can be viewed as a natural occurrence, a simple by-product of our lives without any sinister implications. Examples like the desire for the sustenance of food and water, sufficient rest and a sense of happiness and well-being for ourselves and our families are of course quite normal and unobtrusive. Even the desire for sex arises naturally in beings that must procreate to ensure the survival of their species, even though that desire may not be consciously linked to procreation at all.

For me, craving is inordinate, almost unnatural. It takes a natural desire and spins it, magnifies it through personal or cultural tales of what might be, what should be, if only we could orchestrate it and hold on to it. If we could mold desire, amplify it, make it fit the story we have made of it, then we might know true pleasure, true happiness, true fulfillment. Then, like a knight and his princess riding off into the sunset, we might, at long last, live happily ever after. And if not here, then in some Valhalla that rewards valiant warriors, some heaven that rewards those whose beliefs are religiously correct, or some realm where pliant virgins await martyrs. Seventy-two, I believe, is the exact number.

Craving signifies desire gone mad. It is a grasping tension beyond natural instinct that infuses biological desire with a story concocted by the dualistic human intellect, producing in the end a story whose ending is more fiction that fact, more conducive to disappointment than satisfaction.

Likewise, a distinction between pain and suffering can also be carefully drawn, although in common understanding they are often lumped together. As desire is more natural than craving, pain is more inevitable than suffering. Pain occurs naturally as a result of illness and injury, both physical and emotional. Suffering is our reaction to it, our story about it. Suffering is our mental craving to hold to pleasure with all our might and avoid life's pain at all cost.

Buddha teaches that in truth it is this craving, this grasping tension that causes suffering. The fact that the reality of natural desire does not fit the fantasies we create about it is a problem of our own construction. The inescapable truth that beings are born and die, that we are ill and grow old, that we cannot seem to hold on to anything we have, this is merely the natural flow of matter and energy. This is because life is actually…ALIVE! Life is movement, it is flow. How could something that must flow ever remain steady or fixed? The river of life does not flow with metal that can be cast in the molds of our own creation. Like all rivers, it runs with water and the firmer our grasp, the quicker it seeps away. It is the clinging to our fairytale stories of existence that causes our suffering, and as we have seen, these stories arise from an inadequate appreciation of the true nature of our existence.

The Third Noble Truth is usually expressed, "…with the cessation of desire we can bring an end to suffering." And the

Fourth Noble Truth directs us to Buddha's Eightfold Noble Path, a path of ceaseless practice with skillful means as the way to put an end to desire.

Again, I think it is critical that a distinction be made between simple, natural desires and the cravings and attachments that evolve from them in the human psyche. A superficial appreciation of this basic teaching can do more harm than good. If you were to hear this teaching, and then go off by yourself and attempt to put an end to your desire, you might spend years striving to stifle the desire that naturally arises as part and parcel of being alive.

Hui-neng (Jap. Eno) 638-713 CE, known as the sixth patriarch of Zen in China, is considered the father of Zen. For there emerged in his teaching a combination of the wisdom of Chinese Taoism with the Buddhist tradition from India creating something unique which has survived to the modern era. He is the author of the Platform Sutra, the only work given the status of sutra since the time of Shakyamuni Buddha himself. But in his sutra, Hui-neng emphatically claims that, "...the very passions themselves are enlightenment."

This statement seems at first glance to contradict the usual translation of Buddha's teaching that it is desire itself that causes suffering. How could something that causes suffering be synonymous with enlightenment? But if you'll recall our discussion of enlightenment earlier, the Zen tradition speaks of it as, "...the absolute light, luminous throughout the whole universe; unfathomable excellence penetrating everywhere..." Given this appreciation, how is it possible for desire to be excluded?

My first teacher, the Rinzai Master Osaka Koryu Roshi, was once asked by a student, "Should I purify my desire?" Koryu Roshi's reply was simply, "No. *Refine* your desire." This is the best teaching on desire I've ever heard, and in one sharp dagger thrust it cuts through the delusion that somehow desire must be extinguished. Ultimately, we *are* desire, an energy that pulses through the universe, manifesting as the life we are and the life we see. We use fire to cook our food, but it is the same fire that burns down the forest. In one instance we call it good, in another, bad. It is the way in which it is used that eventually creates the story of suffering, or what I consider its opposite, well-being.

A basic tenet of Buddhist teaching is that pain is inevitable but suffering is optional. It is our response to pain that creates our suffering. As human animals on this planet, we are naturally subjected to the ebb and flow of life which tugs constantly at the fabric of our lives. This, at times, results in understandable and inevitable pain. Yet it is also true that we are attached to an ego concept that continually validates itself as separate from the world. One way it does this is through the simple process of craving and aversion that arises largely from our personal and cultural beliefs. We are prone to take the natural ups and downs of life personally. We take the good times, the successes, as proof of either personal superiority or a kind God, and bad times and failures as indicative of our personal failings or abandonment by a supreme being. All animals love pleasure and avoid pain. But when was the last time you saw a wounded animal raise its paw toward heaven, curse God and ask, "Why?"

In the human animal, this process has evolved into the ego's yearning for the mental reinforcement of its own identity, and a rejection of anything that undermines this most cherished delusion, cherished even though it can easily turn modest pain into suffering. Zen practice aims at freeing students from this tiring mental gymnastic, and its associated trauma, so that they might truly relax into their own original natures.

But there's more to it. Buddha himself was born as Prince Siddharta and was raised in the castle of his father, the king, and shielded from any contact with the pains of the poor. It wasn't until after he was married and had a son that he ventured outside the castle for the first time and witnessed sickness, old age and death. He was so overwhelmed by the power of this suffering that he set out to find an answer.

My point is that before he witnessed pain, the Buddha had no story of suffering. Would he ever have set out on his quest if he'd never witnessed the pain of existence? Our problem is not only the result of an ego concept. It is also a plethora of unaddressed pains that creates the general story of suffering. This too is the valid purview of Zen.

Dealing with suffering from the angle of ego attachment is a wonderful skillful means. But dealing with the pain directly and honestly is also invaluable, especially for the modern layman. And meditation is an invaluable tool not only for releasing the delusion of the separate self, it is also valuable for removing the veil of the story we create about our pain and uncovering the very wisdom of the pain itself.

Nicolee Jikyo McMahon Roshi, my wife, offers a teaching on suffering brilliantly equivalent and wonderfully complimentary to that of Koryru Roshi. She teaches that when Buddha said that life is suffering and desire is the cause of that suffering, that he was not making a value judgment that somehow we've failed if our desires cause us suffering. It was a statement of fact. Suffering is information. Nicolee Roshi encourages us to inquire into the information that our suffering holds. So when we are suffering, we can ask our suffering what is wanted. For example, in the beginning of this chapter, I discussed a relationship that had turned sour. The pain from my lost relationship wanted, among other things, control. If we go a step further, Nicolee Roshi asks how long would I have wanted control? And, if I were telling the truth, I would have said, "...for as long as possible." Because everything is changing all the time, my desire for control would continue to cause me suffering. By becoming aware of this, I can free myself from continuing to generate more pain. Seeing, over and over, into the relationship between suffering, desire and *time* is one of the great teachings of Buddhism. It is not wrong to have desire or to suffer, but there *is* a clear relationship. There's also nothing wrong with craving, but its relationship to our suffering must be clearly appreciated if we are to have any skill in dealing with it.

We talked in the previous chapter about the nature of time and our experience of its flow, and how that common experience of the flow of time from past to present to future had no absolute basis in physics. But the practice of Zen enables us to experience not only this absolute perspective of what is called the eternal *NOW*, but also helps us appreciate more fully and more practically the relative aspect of time's ceaseless mutation. Master Dogen emphasizes that we are not separate from time, but that we *are* time. And the fleeting nature of our existence is not only something we observe, it is truly something that we *are*. The realization of emptiness teaches us that there is truly nothing to hold to, and no one to hold it. Our True Nature entails an absolute reality that contains and infuses our relative world with the energy and wisdom to live and die according to cause and effect, in perfect synchronicity, as brilliant as it is ungraspable. Realizing this, we can accept the inevitable pleasure and pain, joy and suffering of life as part of what we truly are, the flow of existence, and all its seeming opposites, manifesting on a momentary basis as our life. But to do this, we need to realize both the wisdom of our desires, and our unity with time itself.

I know many people who are generally unhappy a great deal of the time yet have no understanding as to why. They've never learned to allow the natural wisdom of their own inner life, their pains and desires, to free them of the proverbial straightjacket they've inherited and don't even know they're wearing. Addressing our own inner pains and desires is not selfish; it is vital in developing an honest sense of self and healthy mode of living. It contributes positively to the whole world. As one guru put it, the best gift you can give the world is a healthy and happy you.

I deal with desire, and even the so-called negative emotions like anger or fear, in the following way: I welcome them. Without them, I would be lost. It is the wisdom by which I live. It arises from the flow of intelligence and information that is the life of each one of us.

When I was flying in the Gulf of Sidra during our freedom of navigation disputes with Libya in the early 1980s, I carried under my wing a heat-seeking infrared missile known as the AIM-9L. Once the seeker head of the missile acquired the target, usually the hot engine of the enemy aircraft, it would compute a lead collision course to the target to control its own flight path to intercept. Once this flight path was computed, the missile would fly its intercept course purely, and, absent evasive moves by the target aircraft, the missile would see no need to change anything and fly directly to intercept without correction. But while doing so, the seeker head would remain completely open to any information about the infrared signature of the target aircraft. That is, should the target change speed or course, the seeker head would immediately accept this new information, this change, and recalculate its course. In other words, if the missile saw and felt nothing, it knew its course was true yet remained at all times open to any information that may require a change in course. I use this analogy to talk about desire and our lives.

The missile's seeker-head displayed openness and adaptability to change that made it one of the most effective in history. Its system was truly like a mirror, reflecting equally all the information before it, neither holding to nor rejecting anything from preconceived notions, yet reacting freely and instantly. Can we not naturally do that as well? Can we not use all the instinctive and emotional information we receive to refine our own course through life?

Of course, we humans are not machines, yet we are not without programming. Our cultural programming allows us to live together in the social groups in which we find ourselves. But many of our conditioned attachments and cravings are programmed as part of an accepted and unchallenged cultural, political and economic ethos, as part of our basic human legacy. Although not *wrong,* if the dynamic is not clearly understood, we are forced to slog through sufferings of our own creation, through the traumas of our own battlefields.

Meditation and Desire

Those who meditate, especially in a long retreat, will generally arrive at a state of mind that exhibits true balance. A beginner, or even a more advanced student in the first day or two of a retreat, may see an endless stream of mind junk flowing through their conscious minds. But as the student continues to meditate, they will experience a mind that is settled. It is similar to one of those crystal balls with the winter home and fake snow that after it is shaken and allowed to sit will eventually clear itself merely because it is allowed to remain in stillness.

The traditional term for a Zen retreat is *sesshin*, which literally means *to gather the mind*. Here we experience a gathering of the mind's power that is no longer scattered by the busyness of daily life, but rather is allowed to experience its own innate stillness, balance, vastness and harmony. When the mind is agitated, the world is at war. When the mind is gathered, the world is at peace. Yet even into this cave of deep meditation it is not unusual for thought, desire or anxiety to naturally arise. The causes vary and are dependent upon the individual's age, practice and current life situation among a host of other things. The factors are actually too vast to comprehend, but it is a mistake to assume that they arise due solely to a lack of skillful meditation or enlightened understanding.

It is true that advanced meditators may experience less disruption due to their dedicated practice. They may also experience no disruption at all. It is also true that the level of one's understanding can come into play and that advanced practitioners may more easily, indeed effortlessly, let go of random mind states that may cause a less experienced students undue anxiety.

In the setting described above, we can even appreciate that desire does not cause pain so much that it *is* pain. In the midst of this deep cave of meditation, silently sitting and gently breathing through this timeless body, like kelp softly swaying at the bottom of clean, fresh sea, a desire may suddenly arise, like a knot in the stomach, destroying this wonderful peace. It is impossible for us to understand all the reasons that cause emotions to arise, but far from being a sign of poor practice or inadequate understanding, perhaps it is a voice that needs to be heard. Perhaps there's an honest, unmet need that will keep speaking until it is addressed, like a small child that cries until its parents respond.

Zen Buddhists don't just appreciate the empty space of deep meditation; they appreciate everything that arises from it, as well. Without exception, it is the voice of Buddha, the wisdom of life. In the Prajnaparamita Sutra, Buddha states, "…Prajnaparamita (the perfection of wisdom) unveils all phenomena, all structures of relativity, as the boundless expanse of openness and luminous transparency." In the *Book of Equanimity*, a classic of the Zen tradition, it states that after enlightenment, "…all throughout the universe, everything becomes food."

Thoughts and desires, even cravings and aversions, arise like clouds floating through the vast sky of your own mind. Like the clouds that coalesce from the heat and moisture of the sky, all states of mind have their origin in the essence of Mind itself, vast, unknowable and without hindrance. And like the clouds in the summer sky, they arise, transform and disappear of their own accord, on a time scale dictated by the vast universal web of cause and effect. In Buddhist understanding, this is the functioning of wisdom, even though our meager human interpretations constantly find reason for complaint. It is not because we lack for anything that we suffer. It is because we do not listen, we do not understand and we do not appreciate what is readily available as the guiding wisdom of our lives. And that wisdom is precisely what manifests as the stream of information arising as our thought, our desire, our fear and our anger. It is only because the habitual, conditioned intellect refuses to accept the information that a constant tension arises between the reality that we are, and the illusion that we insist on creating.

The Clear Light
In the beginning of this chapter, I described my attachment to a girl in my youth. In retrospect, I can only make sense of it by attempting to view it in the broadest sense possible, like an official boarding a plane to fly over a disaster area in order to get a comprehensive view.

Like any experience in life, it is composed of a variety of forces, just as a rope is made of many strands of fiber, and in an attempt to apply the salve of understanding to ease my suffering, I feel I must carefully unwind each strand to view it separately and appreciate its contribution to the whole mess.

There was an initial condition of loneliness and boredom. Then there was a physical attraction to a young woman whose personality was cheerful and appealing, at least at first. A relationship developed that soon turned sour. How could she not want me? As a fighter pilot with a good reputation, I was on top of the world, handsome and invincible. Or so I thought. My ego locked me into a vain struggle against her rejection. Forlorn at her loss, overjoyed at her return, I was like the village drunk, grateful for any emotional handouts from her to keep me intoxicated enough to string along. For her, it was fun. A game. For me, the only fun part was the pride that came before the fall. But fall I did.

But there was no single strand that could possibly have made this rope, this noose around my neck. The impetus of loneliness, the pulse of sexual desire, the arrogance of youthful success and male power; all these combined to create my demise. And from my own family and strict Catholic upbringing, I inherited no wealth of valuable information on how to deal with women, with sex, with relationships. I felt like a novice recruit, poorly trained and sent to the front toting a rifle without ammunition. So here, plainly, and for all to see, was desire, craving, attachment, pain and suffering.

But now that the rope is being unwound with its strands laid bare, what can we appreciate? The simple need, the pure desire is unmistakable. We are primates by origin and nourished by interaction with other human beings, other vibrant nervous systems. In my case, this arises as joy in sharing life with my wife, in family gatherings, competitive manly company in sports, friendly reminisces with old friends in the Navy and from school and with those engaged in Zen. When it comes to relationships, as a heterosexual I've always been attracted to women, although below the waist and above the neck have never quite understood each other.

But I believe we seek a relationship with the opposite sex to find completeness and to support that aspect of ourselves that we little comprehend and less know what to do with. So a relationship is not only for sex or for biological procreation, but in its best sense it provides what we all seek: complimentary and harmonious interaction with another center of energy and information that provides support, nourishment and solace. It is a jewel that we could never find alone.

But in the progression from the sustenance of natural desire to the sufferings of craving and attachment, there is seldom a clear line of demarcation. It is not a large demilitarized zone between opposing camps. It is more like the subtle, overlapping lines we see on a beach after a receding tide, more like driving between two states. Without a sign posted you'd have no idea you'd crossed the border.

There is a sense we all have of ourselves, a relative sense of self that combines innate personal traits, human neurological inheritance and social conditioning. The eagerness of males to compete for dominance is as easily seen in a wolf pack or lion pride as it is in a group of boys on a football field. The alpha male wins the right to procreate with all the females of his species, the football hero gets to date the prettiest cheerleader. But in advanced human societies these basic biological traits have evolved into deeply imbedded stories of what a *man should be* if he is to be successful, if he is to be *happy*. If he wins on the gridiron, he gets a trophy. If he's brave on the battlefield, he gets a medal. Heroes are always heroes. Social reinforcement solidifies an individual's sense of self, his ego concept. This is as true for the coward or villain as it is for the hero. We seek a role and we play a role. Whether good or bad doesn't really matter for it gives us a way to *know* ourselves and our *place* in the social nexus. The scariest thing for us is letting go, not knowing who we are. But in so doing, we enslave ourselves to stories which ultimately fail the test of reality and induce our suffering.

No one is always strong or always brave. No one is always good or kind. Holding to our stories about who we are may provide a temporary shelter for our sense of self, but they cut us off from the very wisdom that can guide us.

When I flew F-14s off the *USS Nimitz*, I had to make almost 100 night landings on this aircraft carrier at sea. They scared me shitless. I experienced a resistance to them that was extremely uncomfortable. Yet over time, I witnessed something remarkable: if I had to make repeated night landings, called *traps*, in a period of a week, say, my resistance began to ease because my body/mind realized it could now handle the situation with more confidence due to increased exposure to the environment. This fear and resistance was my own body/mind's wisdom, saying, in effect, "You'd better be on your toes." This wisdom heightened all my senses and kept me extremely alert and responsive. The training took over from there, and after repeated night traps, the fear and resistance abated because they were no longer needed. But after a week or so of port call, when it came time for me to fly at night again, the fear and resistance returned, precisely because they were needed once again. If I had fought them, holding to the vain and false story that a true fighter pilot knows no fear, then I would have made an already dangerous situation much worse. I would have blocked the flow of the most needed emotions at the time: fear and resistance. It's not that I don't have fear and resistance. It's rather that I have learned to welcome them as invaluable tools.

If our happiness in life becomes dictated by our success at resembling the many stories we hold to, then we cut ourselves off from the natural wisdom that is readily available to all of us. And the simple yet sure joy of our own existence, in whatever way we find it, is uselessly lost, drowned in a sea of fantasy.

So what does all this have to say about my own predicament in that relationship? Of course, the mere fact that I might seek a relationship with someone has the potential for an honest rejection and subsequent disappointment. But like any other pursuit in life, there is no crime or shame in failure, unless I insist upon it.

But I was at a point in my life where my ego concept was at its strongest. This powerful attachment to whom I thought I was and what was due me on account of my self-appointed status created a tension and an anguish when pitted against the reality of the rejection that I faced. This was not a mere biological drive unrequited. This was a fairy tale with a bad ending I couldn't anticipate or accept. And my lack of acceptance and concomitant suffering was completely self-induced; induced not by a natural desire so much as by the delusion of my own ego story, reinforced by accolades and medals from a society as drunk on its own delusions as I was on mine.

Desire is the clear light that illumines our journey through life. And not just desire, but the rich well of all our impulses and feelings. But they can easily become distorted and perverted by a conditioned concept of self that exacerbates natural and modest pain and turns it into monumental suffering.

Master Dogen (1200-1253 CE) said, "It is Buddhas who enlighten delusion. It is creatures who are deluded in enlightenment." Although common spiritual understanding has often turned desire into some instrument of a malicious devil, Buddhist realization identifies it as an invaluable tool for clarifying and refining our life, the very wind that fills our sails and carries us across the sea of existence.

Jesus said that, "Man does not live by bread alone, but by every word that issues from the mouth of God." For Buddhists, this "every word" is indeed the endless stream of sight, sound, smell, taste, touch and mental formulation. It is all of our biological life and all our emotions. It is all of life within and without us. Who's to say what comes from the mouth of God is wrong?

It's a mistake to assume that what I'm trying to relate is reason to justify all your desires and emotions as being *right*. There is no right or wrong here, merely cause and effect. Much arises within us that should only be noticed without taking action.

I love to surf and I bob up and down on an ocean of endless wave action. All kinds of waves come and I feel every one of them as they flow through me. But I don't ride them all. Some are too small and inconsequential. Some are too big and dangerous. Years of experience and practice have clarified for me the nature of wave dynamics, making me comfortable in a wide variety of surf conditions and teaching me to chose wisely before I try to ride one. I can't avoid feeling them. But I can avoid riding them.

So it is with our desires and emotions. Zen practice helps us do exactly what Koryu Roshi advised. It helps us refine desire and distill its wonderful essence from the potentially harmful effects of the conditioned mind. Once clarified, the decision to move with or let go of any desire or emotion becomes significantly easier. Rather than a lightning quick progression from desire to craving to suffering, we actually have the ability to use the energy of desire to contribute to the overall well-being of ourselves and others.

Changing the Past
In talking about my failed relationship, I used the analogy of a rope around my neck. I tried to emphasize that it takes many different strands to create the rope and that, to understand my suffering, I had to unwind the rope slowly and attempt to identify the many individual strands that wound around each other.

Buddha understood that suffering was intimately woven into the very fabric of our lives. And lacking a sincere effort to understand this suffering and its causes, to unwind the rope, we would be doomed to the ceaseless birth and death of an existence riddled with suffering, a recurring nightmare of our own creation. It's like someone who always seems to end up in a bad relationship no matter how many times he or she walks down the aisle.

In Buddhism, this effort takes the form of meditation, of mindfulness. The practice shines a light on the rope of suffering and its heat softens the fibers so that they may be unwound and viewed. Once this process begins we begin to gain power over the potentially catastrophic functioning of conditioned response. Meditation provides the necessary mental stability and clarity with which we can clearly see the individual strands.

And this practice does more than provide a conscious, liberated life for the present, or even for the future. It actually can change the past. There are modern experiments in physics, called *delayed-choice* experiments, where the observation of a subatomic particle's position in the present seems to have determined that particle's path *in the past*. Bizarre as it may sound, there are numerous experiments in this field initially proposed by the famous physicist John Wheeler in 1980.

Using our analogy of the rope, imagine that you're holding it in the middle and unwinding it on your lap. If you look to your right, you'll see it unravel in that direction. But if you look to your left, it unravels in that direction as well.

Now imagine your practice of meditation, of awareness, reveals to you some suffering particular to your life and the many strands that comprise it. As that understanding, that clarity, unravels and releases the rope of your suffering in the present, it also gives you the power to transform that dynamic for good in the future. But remember, the rope unravels in both directions. Whatever conditioned response created your suffering in the past over countless days, weeks, months or even years could have been the very reason for a ruined life. But now the heat of awareness that you bring to it in the present actually melts the conditioning of the past, and changes the initial condition from a negative foundation for suffering to the very basis of your emancipation. The cold, hard story of your past has now been melted and transformed by the heat of your present illumination, changing the very meaning of those events in the past from a certain cause of suffering to the very reason for your present liberation.

My own suffering with the girl in my youth was a significant point in my understanding of myself, of life and of Zen. Drop by drop from pain is wisdom distilled. For a long while, I could only see it as a great disaster. But the practice of Zen, and the understanding that flows from it, has enabled me to clearly view my own human tendency to exacerbate a modest pain and turn it into a colossal disaster simply by allowing a simple and honest desire to be infected by a conceptually driven intellect. In short, I engineered a debacle where a wholesome motivation became a stake through my heart by holding to a story of who I thought I was, and what I insisted I should have. Life did not make me suffer so. I did it to myself.

Suffering is important because it teaches us, if we are willing to learn, how the human mind endeavors to cram the vital functioning of life into the narrow stories it constructs, with unintended yet damaging results. In one way, it's a curse. But it is also important to realize that suffering is a blessing as well, because it can propel us mortals toward realizing our innate Buddhahood. Suffering, and the great doubt about human existence it instills, is the one force that can propel us toward an understanding of a life beyond doubt, buoyed and illuminated by the clear light. It is an understanding that is readily available to all of us, yet whose lack has plagued humankind since the dawn of human consciousness.

Chapter Seven

THE DEVIL'S ADVOCATE
The Importance of Natural Instinct and Well-Being

"Think about it. He (God) gives man instincts! He gives this extraordinary gift and then what does He do? I swear for His own amusement, His own cosmic gag reel, He sets the rules in opposition. It's the goof of all time! Look, but don't touch! Touch, but don't taste! Taste, but don't swallow! And while you're down here jumping from one foot to the next, He's laughing His sick fucking ass off!"

—Al Pacino as John Milton (The Devil)
In *The Devil's Advocate* novel by Andrew Neiderman, screenplay by Jonathan Lemkin

Somehow, human beings have evolved a conceptual dynamic that pits us against ourselves, against the very instincts that have allowed us to survive. We grudgingly acknowledge our animal natures even while many philosophies and religious traditions encourage a rejection of the instinctual urges as somehow the work of the Devil. Accepting this inherited belief without question puts us on a track of ceaseless tension between what are undeniable instincts on the one hand, and the struggle to control their expression on the other. It is indeed, the goof of all time.

But is the animal kingdom devoid of restrictions to natural instinct? I am not an expert on what internal controls animals may exercise on their own instincts. Simple observation does not seem to indicate much in this regard, but it would be foolish to claim they have none. But nature herself puts restrictions on them. For example, alpha males in several species control sexual access to females, leaving lesser males out of the loop unless they can grab a little on the side without Papa knowing. I even saw in one instance a pack of monkeys loudly alerting the alpha male that one of his ladies was having a little affair in a thicket while he was asleep. Papa awoke and took off after the offending pair and delivered a sound beating. This obvious type of risk/reward scenario is probably enough to evolve internal controls of some sort on various species.

However, one thing seems certain: to our knowledge, the animal kingdom has not developed extensive intellectual constructs that justify the restriction of natural instinct, sending the compliant to a promised paradise and the offending to a dreaded hell realm. To my observation, the absence of this justification makes them more at home with themselves and their environment. They try to eat if they're hungry, sleep when they're tired, copulate when they can and don't seem to browbeat themselves for doing so. To my knowledge, animal experts in the field have yet to witness self-flagellation.

The presence of this rationalization in humans, the need to restrain natural instinct, while an expedient means to control large numbers of people, can have the unintended result of producing an unnatural anxiety and discomfort deep within ourselves. This is low self-esteem in its most basic sense, and the deeply ingrained fissure, the gap between the intellectual idea we create of ourselves and the reality of our own innate organic existence produces, on an ascending scale, unease, fear, anger and unnecessary conflict. And with this schism deep in our minds and hearts, developing an intelligent response to natural instinct and finding a true sense of well-being in this life becomes nearly impossible.

There is an ancient symbol for this idea of well-being used by Eastern cultures which originated more than 3,000 years ago. It derives from the Sanskrit term, *svasti*, which means *conducive to well-being* or *happiness*. What surprises us, especially in the West, is that this symbol is the swastika. This swastika could be seen in both left facing and right facing forms long before the Nazis adopted the right facing symbol during their rise to power. But it is safe to say that the original meaning was lost by the Nazis who used it to symbolize something vastly different.

How is it that, over time, the human mind turned a symbol for well-being into a symbol that became associated with suppression and destruction? How, and indeed why, does the human intellect distort natural instinct and turn it into a perversion? Zen would answer that it is simply the result of delusion. Being blinded to our True Nature, our Buddha Nature, the universality we share with all of life, propels us to identify with ever more bizarre intellectual constructs to bolster this false sense of ourselves, with an endless cycle of suffering as our reward.

In Zen there is an old saying that mimics what I previously said about animals, "Eat when you're hungry, sleep when you're tired." This may sound like an intelligent response to natural instinct and a nice recipe for well-being. But it is used in Zen not because it is an unrealistic panacea that addresses mere physical comfort, but because it radiates from a deep appreciation of the wisdom inherent in life itself, a wisdom that germinates everywhere naturally, and prior to the inevitable and habitual intellectual distortion that the human mind can imprint on natural instinct. And this distortion is symbolized ultimately in the Nazi perversion of the original swastika.

The practice of Zen is highly disciplined. No one in a Zen monastery has the luxury of eating when hungry or sleeping when tired. The discipline is similar to that of the military where a strict training schedule is observed. On the surface, it seems a great contradiction. But my teacher, Tenshin Roshi, explained it to me with the Buddhist symbol of the swastika. In a Buddhist temple, paper replicas of right facing symbols would blow counter-clockwise in the wind. This symbolized that practice often goes, against the grain, as it were, an artificial necessity. But once this training produced true understanding, it was like turning the symbol around so that it could go clockwise, in harmony with the grain, or wind.

In other words, without understanding, it's hard to know what natural behavior might truly be. This can be seen by the propensity of many of us to act in ways totally contrary to our own well-being even in our free time. We get so alienated from our own natural instincts after decades of living by the clock that we need drugs to go to sleep and drugs to wake up. We need drugs to go to the toilet and drugs to stop us from going just so we can make it through that all-important meeting. And thanks to the miracle of modern medicine, we can even use drugs to get an erection! (But remember that erections lasting more that 24 hours should seek immediate medical attention.) I'm not sure I'll need a hard-on in my coffin.

As one retiree once told me, "I have all this free time now and I want to do what I want to do. But I don't know what I want to do." It's often sad but true that after you've lived in a cage for so many years, you have no idea what to do with yourself when they let you out.

In the previous chapter, I made a distinction between pain and suffering, and between desire and craving. I attempted to reveal the thin line between the natural and instinctual realities of life and the way in which the conditioned human intellect can distort their inherent wisdom and produce suffering. I discussed both the aspect of letting go of our habitual and conceptual ego structures as well as responding positively to the natural instincts that are part and parcel of life.

For me, the opposite of suffering is not so much joy as it is well-being. And it involves not just the physical, but the mental and emotional states, as well. *Well-being* is a vague concept, like *truth* or *justice*. They are vague because they entail a combination of realities, or energies, that coalesce into a recognizable feeling or perception in the present moment. But with the loss of any pillar, the whole temple can come crumbling down. I may be healthy, but my doubt torments me. I may be intelligent, but poverty has caused my family to suffer. I may be wealthy, but emotional dysfunction has led to several divorces. I was content, but now my child is dying and I want to die, too.

We're only as strong as our weakest link. We cannot control what life deals us, but we can practice to avoid foolish choices. Well-being is ephemeral, yet genuine. It's as fleeting as a summer rain, but equally as nourishing. It arises naturally when body, heart and mind are in balance. And this balance brings peace.

But what about spiritual well-being? Is there such a thing? Once, on a bitterly cold December day, I walked past a beggar in the streets of Boston. He was physically incapacitated, in a wheelchair and seemingly retarded. I gave him some money and stopped to chat. He saw the sad look on my face and said, "Don't feel sorry for me. I have…" there he paused a long beat before smiling and saying, "…everything!"

What inner treasures had he uncovered that made him content amidst all his afflictions? It is undeniable that a deep spiritual place of rest is found by some who transcend the many maladies they suffer. It is a great gift. And it is true that meditation and deep spiritual experience often transcend our normal physical, mental and emotional sensations. Yet this very transcendence, this enlightenment, also opens us to the very wisdom of those same sensations and energies, for their voice is no longer hidden behind a veil of illusory separation or distorted by intellectual fabrication. As I mentioned in the last chapter, the Sixth Patriarch of Zen, Hui-neng, exclaimed that, "…the very passions themselves are enlightenment."

Still, many of us who are free from physical and mental hindrances stumble blindly through dark alleys of suffering without reason. Zen has traditionally identified the cause of our suffering as delusion and aimed the arrow of its practice and realization straight at delusion's heart. True understanding has the power of dissolving the corrosive aspects of delusion and freeing the student from doubt and suffering. In zazen, as our minds become unified through practice, the ceaseless waves of mental activity become stilled and we begin to have greater access to an original wholeness, ease and comfort that is the very foundation of well-being. Master Dogen called zazen, "…the dharma gate of ease and joy." When inside and outside are naturally merged and the usual sense of self drops away, true balance and harmony are naturally realized.

Yet Zen emphasizes the impermanence of everything, including mental states of…*ease and joy*, and the danger of holding to any particular state of mind, which can quickly become its own hindrance. But even though these states are transitory, it doesn't mean they're not valuable. When I surf a great wave, I know that wonderful experience of flow is over quickly, yet, that understanding does not prevent me from riding them for I know from experience the great value of that fleeting glide. All experience is impermanent. And that is precisely why, from the very beginning, life is liberation itself. Although all states are fleeting, these waves of experience determine the very quality of our lives, and our choices are critical in determining the character of our existence. We may feel them all, but we don't have to ride them all.

When Buddha himself talked about the Eight Awarenesses of the enlightened person, he began them with two very important ones pertinent to our discussion here. The first was *have few desires,* and the second was *know how to be satisfied*. Food is a necessity, but gorging ourselves causes illness and pain. Sleep is regenerative, but too much of it makes us groggy and ineffective. Sex is central to all species, yet exaggerated emphasis on it as a means to sell everything from soap to cars to pornography probably generates as much dysfunctional behavior as it does cash. But the more our natural instincts are clarified and addressed wisely, the easier it becomes to truly know how to be satisfied, even though this satisfaction will take many forms for different people.

Selfish or Selfless? "I Only Drink the Best"

Buddhism has *precepts* that, at first reading, may sound similar to Christian commandments. But Christian commandments are often appreciated as laws that, if violated, are sins that displease a Superior Being and can land us in eternal punishment. Buddhist precepts, on the other hand, as one Japanese Zen Master told me, are really meant to protect us so that we can practice and realize. They are meant to release us from suffering here and now.

A few years ago, I was visiting a very old Japanese Master named Chido Roshi, who, although a layman, received dharma transmission from two famous masters, Joko Roshi and Yamamoto Gempo Roshi. Chido Roshi was a dharma brother of my first teacher, Osaka Koryu Roshi. Chido Roshi told me that once he asked Yamamoto Gempo, "How do you maintain the precepts?" Gempo Roshi replied, "When I drink, I only drink the best!" At a later time, Chido then asked Koryu Roshi the same question, to which Koryu replied, "I only bow to myself."

A superficial appreciation of these responses might lead us to think that these masters were promoting drunkenness and even self-centeredness. But this is far from their intent. There is a profound spiritual meaning that these words would have for Zen Masters whose lifetime of practice had truly clarified for them the nature of *self*, and the spiritual implications of what the phrase *drinking the best*, would imply. But their answers also indicate a high degree of the refinement of decision and action on a personal level, especially for men steeped in a highly civilized society and disciplined practice whose main goal has often been categorized in the West by the largely misunderstood term *self-effacement* or *selflessness*. If ultimately there is no *self*, then what is there to be effaced? If the *self* is an illusion, why does it hold such an immense power over us?

I once had a dream as a child where a dog was biting me, and I knew I was dreaming, but I couldn't understand why it still hurt even though I was aware that it was all a dream. When I awoke, I realized that the pain was coming from the fact that my arm somehow had gotten stuck under my torso in an awkward twist. No matter what our level of understanding or our awareness might be, pain and suffering often arise from causes beyond any possible capacity of perception. Pain in life is inevitable. Buddhism deals with the way in which human suffering arises from the unskillful way in which we deal with it.

The most basic unskillful means is the inherited chain of dualism, the illusion of self. Neurologically inherited and culturally conditioned, this mental framework permeates our lives and links us inexorably to the sufferings of the past and the future. This is dealt with through the practices of Zen and its realization. The realization that there is, in reality, no separation at all between what we know as the self, and the rest of life, indeed, the understanding that we *are* all of life and that *all* of life is contained in us, is the very basis of this well-being. With this understanding, we are able to view our personal limited tendencies from a broader lens. We can clearly see how we exacerbate our own suffering by dealing with the basic pains of life more like a child than an adult, more like a drunk than a sober person. Yamamoto Gempo Roshi said, "...I only drink the best." Of course in Zen, it's *all* the best. This statement can be taken as a proclamation of his understanding, like the koans of old. And, as such, it's a wonderful reply. He truly drinks in all of life and finds it to be the best.

But, more specifically, Gempo Roshi might indeed have been talking about alcohol, or sake. It is said that he loved to drink. I like to toss a few back myself at times. I've learned over much time (and too much drinking) that fine alcohol not only tastes good and makes me feel fine but also often spares me the hangover, while cheap booze can make me feel sick right from the start. Do not think this is trivial. In talking about alcohol, he's actually addressing the way in which we cheat ourselves by our choices: by going for the cheap instead of the fine, by withholding effort even for a promising goal, by accepting the illusion of short-term ease over the possibility of true peace, stability and harmony on both a personal, national and global level. It's as basic as the way we sit and as grand as the way nations relate.

Selfless or Selfish? "I Only Bow to Myself"
Koryu Roshi's reply to Chido Roshi's query as to how he maintained the precepts was equally intriguing. "I only bow to

myself." Many Buddhists would like to feel that he's talking about the big SELF, Buddha, the Absolute, which feeds his very life, which indeed, *is* his very life. But there is really no difference between little self and so-called big SELF. Bowing to one is bowing to the other. And really, who's bowing? To paraphrase Master Dogen, only Buddha bows to Buddha.

But remember that a Japanese master is steeped in an oriental and Confucian culture where self-effacement, or selflessness, is a highly valued religious, social and even political attribute. A Zen master is thought of as the epitome of that philosophy. So how could a Japanese master seem to go against that ethos and bow, of all things, to himself?

The average person's understanding of this self is as superficial in the East as it is in the West. Most people on both sides of the globe interpret selflessness as something akin to the subordinate relationships of Confucian ethics, or a samurai cutting his guts out for lord or emperor. An average citizen in the Far East no more appreciates Koryu Roshi's Zen than your average Christian in the West understands Thomas Aquinas.

I taught English for a time at a bank in Tokyo. Many of the young executives were given six months off from their usual jobs to study English at Sophia University on a daily basis. I met them once a week for pure conversational practice. But since Sophia was a Catholic university, these young executives had a two-week break over the Christmas holiday, so they decided to go to Hawaii. But when their boss at the bank got wind of it, he forced them to cancel their reservations. He told them that since no one else in the bank would be off for those two weeks, that they could not go to Hawaii. Mind you, they did not have to come into work. They just couldn't go to Hawaii.

I had a class with them that same day and they were visibly upset. But, still, they understood and accepted it. Imagine a boss in the U.S. trying to force his employees to do the same thing. In the Far East in general, and in Japan specifically, the value placed on conformity in the social nexus and their preeminence over individual desire, will and even life stand in stark contrast to Western mores. Eastern religions, including Zen Buddhism, are often used as the philosophical rationale supporting this cultural ethos. Since this ethos teaches that the self is ultimately an illusion, and only the Absolute is real, there is deep support for such ancient traditions as Buddhist and Confucian idealism, samurai loyalty, and bank teller vacation cancellation.

The famous Catholic theologian Hans Kung has criticized Buddhism's teaching of no-self as one of the main causes for the historical abuse of human rights in the Far East. And it is true that a superficial appreciation of its teaching has been used as the philosophical rationale for social interactions that we in the West would now call abusive. We have generally viewed Eastern culture as placing more emphasis on social harmony at the expense of individual freedoms, and the religious teachings of Buddhism and Confucianism as providing the philosophical justification for the individual's total acquiescence to the hierarchical structure in which he or she finds themselves.

I remember returning to Japan after a twenty-year absence and being appalled at the physical congestion and emotional restriction of Tokyo. I felt so constricted and uncomfortable that I couldn't believe I'd actually lived there for five years in my early 20s practicing Zen. But after a few days I noticed something else. I began to see that Japan's emphasis on proper behavior and acceptance of one's status in the hierarchical system provided an enviable smoothness and livability in an area like Tokyo that was crammed with over 12 million people, more than 5,600 people per square kilometer. At the same time, the fact that this harmony is largely superficial and the suppression of individual emotion comes with a physical price tag is evidenced by the fact that Japan has one of the highest rates of stomach cancer in the world. As we used to say in fighter tactics, there's no such thing as a free lunch. Every coin has two sides.

Since the dawn of human society, there has been an uneasy truce between social convention and individual biological necessity. But taking care of one's own being, and the fluctuating nature of our physical, mental and emotional aspects, is not self-centered or selfish. It's a necessity not only for ourselves but for the society in which we thrive. We've all seen people burn themselves out in devotion to a practice or a cause, and though admirable, often the resulting dissolution of their own well-being fans out through the group like a wildfire, causing much damage and perhaps the destruction of what was once a worthy effort.

And while we have at times tended to view the samurai ethic of Japan as the epitome of military discipline and therefore strength (the Tom Cruise film, *The Last Samurai* being one example), the shortsightedness of this myth has even been evident on the battlefield. During the pivotal battle for

Henderson Airfield on the island of Guadalcanal, an elite Japanese Army unit, in wave after wave, charged U.S. Marine machine gun positions headlong and were completely destroyed. The Marines, while impressed with their foes' courage, were shocked at their stupidity. A simple flanking maneuver might have turned the tide for them since the Marines were outnumbered. In this instance at least, the Japanese samurai spirit was more concerned with proving their worth as courageous warriors than in achievement of the military objective. Sacrificing themselves in that way fulfilled their cultural fantasy, but did not provide any success in battle. Indeed, it inhibited success. As General Patton said, "No poor son of a bitch ever won a war by dying for his country. He won it by making the other poor son of a bitch die for his."

But we in the West should not be smug here. We have our own follies to contend with. It is true that at least since the ancient Greeks we have placed a high value on the individual soul, and that basic premise has evolved over time to become individual rights. Our own religious traditions have engraved this in our psyches so much that our heroes are not 47 ronin, selfless samurai committing suicide for the honor of their lost lord, but John Wayne, Clint Eastwood and a host of Hollywood others, slaughtering scores of bad guys who get in the way of one man's intentions. The fact that they are generally seen as defending the weak against the corrupt does not alter the fact that they fulfill our cultural fantasy. The individual, outnumbered, overcomes all odds and rises alone on the winner's platform to accept his award, fulfilling the dream of life, liberty and all the concomitant dough and sexual attention that goes with it. The pursuit of happiness is complete.

American bank tellers can go on their vacations as long as they don't get shot leaving the office. We cannot hide from the dark side of our own ethos because, in the end, our arrogant emphasis on the individual has produced a society where we all feel like innocent loners against all odds. Road rage and school shootouts are but the inevitable result.

So what did Koryu Roshi mean when he said that he only bowed to himself? There is only one self, or Self, which functions and bows, which moves and flows. He honored the wisdom that is essentially his own, and everyone's. Its natural functioning is evident everywhere. When the rain falls, the grass grows. When the sun shines, the flowers blossom. And when your stomach churns, you head to the fridge. Like Yamamoto Gempo, he knew that suffering could easily ensue as a natural by-product of foolish activity, either mental, physical or emotional, that arises from not appreciating fully the wisdom of this Self and allowing oneself to be unconsciously dragged along in the stream of conditioned response.

A life intelligently lived is what we all seek, and we are born with abundant wisdom on how to do just that. Our foolishness lies in our rejection of it. And much of this foolishness can be found in the perversion of natural instinct sacrificed on the altar of cultural conditioning, often nothing more than an agreed upon mass insanity. When all the patients in the asylum nod their heads as one, even shit turns to gold.

The Value of Practice and the Middle Way
When Shakyamuni Buddha first embarked on his search for the truth of existence, he experimented with asceticism,

the most accepted form of spiritual practice of his day. But after years of ascetic practice, he was at the brink of self-annihilation. Then one day, he overheard a man teaching a young boy how to string a lyre. Buddha heard, "If you string it too tight, it will break. If you don't string it tight enough, it won't play." Hearing this freed him from the path he was on. He rejected asceticism and extremism and gave birth to the practice of The Middle Way. And in this practice, and in this Way, a great deal of respect is given to the body and its wisdom because it is ultimately realized that this body is a manifestation of Mind, that Absolute light penetrating everywhere. And balance is an essential ingredient of the power that produces insight and well-being alike, for it is not leaked through the folly and imbalance of physical, mental or emotional disintegration.

Our nervous systems are constructed so that our inner or subjective reality is far more present to our experience than the outward or objective reality we face. In the human body, only one cell in ten thousand filters information from the outside, while the rest are biologically driven and motivated by internal needs such as glandular balance, digestive organization, cleansing apparatus, skin, defecation and others. While this vast internal sensory home is shared by no one but us, we must somehow deal with that outside realm successfully if we are to survive at all. This outside world as it appears to us in human cultural form has its own survival requirements that over long periods of time and for a variety of reasons have transformed into activities ranging from military conscription to Chinese foot binding, from taxes to African neck extensions. Let's face it: the needs of the many have always outweighed the needs of the few.

And I will not be so naïve as to say that only humans act in ways contrary to their own individual well-being. Lemmings may jump off cliffs, and whales may beach themselves, but as far as I know, it's not to get a pat on the back.

I believe that, for us humans, some sort of disciplined practice is invaluable. Indeed, in this life, it is inescapable. If we don't practice with some degree of awareness and intelligent response, we allow ourselves to be dragged into the coalmines of life unwittingly, and cannot avoid suffering as a consequence. Refining the energy of our desires and emotions so that individual satisfaction contributes to, rather than detracts from, the overall well-being of our extended relationships is a practice worthy of a sage, yet open to everyone.

Everywhere we look, people are practicing something. There are Zen students, soldiers, businessmen, doctors, lawyers, actors, teachers, mothers and fathers, all practicing. We can easily see how we often define ourselves by our practice. Yet we all know cases of people who are quite accomplished in their endeavors yet whose personal lives are in a shambles. The reasons are numerous but often boil down to an addictive or conditioned response to life challenges in everything from health to human relationships.

I fly for a major airline, and the physical effects of long hours airborne, all the bad air, bad food and disruptive sleep patterns that go with it are a clear challenge to the health of aircrews. And the results often show up in anger and depression in the people I work with. Yet few seem to appreciate that it's the result of their work. Many are convinced that the cause of their unhappiness is their wives, their kids, the government, taxes or the company. You name it. Many of us are so divorced from our own natural instincts that after years of ignoring the signals of physical, mental and emotional stress we actually believe our own stories that the cause of our unhappiness is…THEM!

My wife works as a therapist and likes to tell the story of a client who was dealing with a lot of stress in his life. Listening to him, she sensed his problems were so overwhelming because of something very basic. She asked him how much water he was drinking and found out that it was almost none. He was perennially dehydrated. When he started drinking an adequate amount of water, he felt strong enough to face the challenges of his life.

Our stories of suffering often arise from a combination of simple pains that are not adequately addressed. Physical, mental and emotional stress unattended to can mount quickly, unobserved, like the sneak attack of a wily foe. Other than a living, breathing being on a changing planet, we become an idea in our own minds, a solid object, a picture on a wall. I once heard a lady emerging from an acupuncturist's office lamenting the fact that she had a body she had to take care of. She said, "I need two bodies. One to take care of, and one to live my life."

I know the stories of yogis who can find a meditative place beyond emotional stress and physical pain. I don't deny it. Anyone who meditates long enough can attest to that. Yet most of us should not be enticed by this. It may be a state one can attain with great practice, yet its immediate value, especially for lay people, does not extend far beyond entertainment.

In Zen, mind and body are *one*. The wisdom of the universe manifests physically. Emptiness *is* form. Our own biological impulses, which are often termed "selfish" by those more interested in our obedience than in our wellbeing, are nothing less than the miraculous intelligence of life pulsating through a body we temporarily call our own. They are not something to regret, abandon, ignore or suppress. They are there to respond to with the wisdom born of a deep appreciation of cause and effect and the interconnectedness of all life. In Buddhism, we realize and appreciate this *one body* of which we are all a part. In a Zen monastery, we take care of it. At home, we take care of it. It's not my body, or yours. It's Buddha's Body. It's Life's Body.

Because of our inability to face the often simple challenges of life openly, honestly and compassionately, we may be condemned to the horror of watching destructive patterns recreate themselves in the sufferings of our children. This is the very basis of samsara, the wheel of birth and death.

Chapter Eight

A TALE OF WELL-BEING
THE IMPORTANCE OF THE MUTINY ON THE BOUNTY

"The world is vast and wide, why do you put on your seven-piece robe at the sound of the bell?"
—Master Ummon (CE 864-949)

"And after all is said and done among us great and wise people of the earth, pray what do we all toil for, late take rest, and eat the bread of carefulness, but to reach, at last, the very state to which they are born…ease of circumstances, and the option of being idle or busy as we please? If I go on this way you will say I am a savage, and so I believe I am, and ever shall be in *some* points…."
—Peter Heywood Midshipman *HMS Bounty* (1772-1831)

The story of the *Mutiny on the Bounty* has fascinated me since I was a child. In it, I believe there is a critical analogy to be found in our quest to unravel the tangled story of human suffering and find a place for well-being. The meeting, or clash, of European and Tahitian cultures that took place in the 18th century has produced a tale that has been retold countless times, providing us with a compelling study of man's ideals and pursuits, and their predictable results.

As a young boy, I remember reading with great interest a book about Captain William Bligh's astonishing survival story after being set adrift with seventeen of his men after the mutiny on his ship *HMS Bounty* in April of 1789. (Interestingly, one of the authors of this book, *Men Against the Sea*, was James Norman Hall, who was a fighter pilot himself in World War I in the famous American volunteer group, the Lafayette Escadrille.) I also remember a great sadness as I watched Marlon Brando, as Fletcher Christian, dying on the beach at Pitcairn Island in the second major film version of that epic tale.

My fascination with this legend has not dimmed even in middle age because in it, I believe, we can find a wonderful correlation between well-being and our struggle with suffering. Suffering is a dilemma that Buddhism has claimed as its *raison d'etre*, and one that I have spent the better part of my life pondering intently.

Life on a military vessel at sea has never been an easy one. Even my own experience with the relative luxury of a modern aircraft carrier filled me with an intense desire to get off it, either by being launched in my F-14 or by marching smartly down the gangway in port. There have even been times in the modern era where seaman have literally jumped off an aircraft carrier in the middle of the open ocean just to put an end to the madness of living in close, cramped quarters with 5,000 other equally disgruntled young men. So you can imagine that life at sea in the British Navy of the late 18th century was no picnic. The punishing patterns of high seas, bad food, irregular sleep, illness, complete lack of privacy and extremely harsh discipline were much worse on the small vessels of the British Navy than they are on today's virtual cities at sea, or love boats, as some like to call them in the modern, gender-integrated Navy.

But attempting to make good time to Tahiti, Bligh aimed for the shortest route around the perilous tip of South America. For almost 30 days, they battled the cold, the sleet, the snow and the highest seas Bligh had ever witnessed.

I was in an Atlantic storm for three days on the large aircraft carrier *USS Nimitz* in the early 1980s. We had 50 - 60 ft. waves washing over the flight deck, turning our jets white with salt, yet the immense size of our ship made the ride really nothing worse than a slow but continual rocking from side to side. But I remember looking out at a much smaller frigate in company with us, and that poor little ship was having the ride of its life, an immense and violent pitching fore and aft as well as port and starboard, with the ocean completely covering its deck at times. How anyone could have even stood up on that vessel in such a storm was beyond me. And they endured it as long as we did, a full three days.

Yet that small frigate was ten times more stable than the little *Bounty* could possibly have been as it futilely pounded its way against the gales off Cape Horn for close to a month, two hundred years earlier. Imagine the life on that ship as a seaman - always cold, always dizzy, always afraid of being washed overboard or falling from the slick, cold masts aloft, always tired and hungry…in short, always miserable. In the end, after 25 days of battle with the sea, the *Bounty* had barely moved a league. It was in basically the same position from which it had started. Bligh finally relented, turned his ship around and made for the Cape of Good Hope, at the tip of South Africa, and a relatively uneventful voyage from there to Tahiti in search of breadfruit to transplant to the West Indies to feed the slaves.

But Tahiti was already well known to the men of the *Bounty* from the stories of previous voyages, and they were eager to experience all the exotic and sensual fantasies those stories had conjured up. And by all accounts, they were not disappointed. Bligh and a few others of his crew had been there before with the famous Captain Cook, and were remembered fondly by the Tahitians.

A utopian vision of Tahitian life had spread in Europe after the French Admiral Bouganville published a glowing account of his visit to the islands in 1767. This account greatly influenced the French philosopher Jean-Jacques Rousseau as he envisaged paradise for his fellow Europeans when he wrote that in such a world, his noble savage would be, "…eating his fill under an oak tree, quenching his thirst at the first stream, making his bed at the foot of the same tree which furnished his meal, with all his needs satisfied." There would be no knowledge of sin, as men had neither vices nor virtues. Living in harmony with nature outside the squalor of cities and the oppressions of large social, political and religious organizations, men and women would finally find happiness and contentment. A paradise on earth.

Of course, no one has ever truly found Rousseau's paradise. Even the Tahitian society of the time was scarred by rivalries and wars, human sacrifice and infanticide. Evolution has always been a competitive endeavor producing winners and losers, elation and agony. A perfect harmony of physical, mental and emotional needs is a fleeting occurrence, an impossible state to maintain. Holding to any state or experience is just another cause of suffering. But that does not discount the fact that in producing agony needlessly, as humans, we are second to none.

One of the reasons well-being is so elusive is that we delude ourselves into rejecting the natural balancing mechanisms of life. We try to overcome fatigue in order to be more productive. We try to forestall old age in order to hold to the illusory joys of youth. We attempt to keep dying patients alive by injecting them with every needle, drug and catheter known to man. Why? So they can suffer longer? If we allowed nature's balancing mechanisms to function more freely, we might get a better sense of peace and equanimity in this life.

Captain Cook took Bligh as his sailing master and introduced him to Tahiti on his third voyage there in 1779. But Cook grew gradually less enamored of the islands. He had grown impatient with the petty thievery of the Tahitians and exacted brutal punishment of the offenders to the extent that even his officers were appalled and grumbled at his behavior in their journals. Cook was also dismayed at their promiscuity and shocked by their practice of infanticide.

Though all utopian fantasies seem to wither in the light of day, nonetheless the stark contrasts of European and Tahitian life were still evident and striking. Many of the early visitors to Tahiti felt they had found Rousseau's paradise; and in all of Cook's three visits to the islands, desertions occurred. An officer on Cook's first voyage, a midshipman named Matra, claimed in later years that a mass desertion had been planned but that he, Matra, had convinced them of its folly. Such was the allure of the islands that indeed desertions were expected.

For the young men of the *Bounty*, fresh off a harsh voyage, it is easy to appreciate their joy at the natural beauty of the island and its people, the mild temperatures, abundant healthy food, and easy sex which welcomed them to the island. But, of course, the attraction of Tahitian life was not just highlighted by comparison to the rough voyage getting there. The men of the *Bounty* were products of a highly regimented society and a Navy that had evolved not just from the traditions of their own country, but also more importantly from the long history of religion, politics and military discipline dating back at least to the ancient Greeks. To put it more succinctly, their sphincters were wired so tight you couldn't pound a toothpick through them with a sledgehammer.

This is not a condemnation. It is the predictable result of societies that evolved in the large landmass of Europe. Tahiti exists in a mild, tropical zone where one could actually live nude year round. For me, there's no vacation like one where I wear nothing but a swimsuit all week, with my surfboard leaning against a thatched hut. This same environment provides easy access to healthy food from the sea and from the land. The small, mountainous islands prevent large populations from taking root, relieving the smaller groups of humans of the necessity of developing the large religious, political and military organizations required to sustain and protect the immense populations that emerged in Europe and Asia.

Large and complex organizations like these must be disciplined if they are to have any value in competition with other societies of similar size and technological advancement. For example, military discipline is required to produce a soldier more efficient in killing than he would otherwise be without it. One of the reasons the Romans were so successful is that they were more disciplined and coordinated than their foes. On an individual basis, no warrior was larger or tougher than a barbarian, but the Romans far exceeded their enemies in discipline and coordination on the battlefield.

The long history of authority, coordination and discipline of military and political organizations that evolved in the large landmasses of Europe and Asia, and the inevitable suppression of natural tendencies it ultimately produced in the young men of the *Bounty*, ran headlong into the languid, relaxed and comfortable lifestyle of Tahiti in October of 1788. The confluence of Western angst and Polynesian ease produced a tale that has been retold in print, in film and even on stage since the 18th century. When Bligh first returned to England after the mutiny, after one of the most harrowing journeys in the annals of the sea, he was met as a hero so deserving that the Royal Theatre produced a play of his exploits entitled, *The Pirates Or, The Calamities of Captain Bligh*. It wasn't until after the court martial of some of the *Bounty's* men apprehended in Tahiti a year and a half later that the public's view of Bligh as hero slowly turned to an image of Bligh as villain. Fletcher Christian, the mutiny's ring leader, and Peter Heywood, a midshipman and close friend of Christian's, had powerful family ties that were very upset that their loved ones were not returned to them safely. It is of interest to note that Fletcher Christian was, in his youth, a schoolmate of the famous poet William Wordsworth, who worked on behalf of Christian's memory in later years. Peter Heywood surrendered in Tahiti and was tried and convicted of mutiny, but received a pardon from the King and eventually returned to naval service.

The mutiny occurred less than a month after the *Bounty* left Tahiti, but the mutineers did not work well together outside the authoritarian system to which they had become accustomed and ultimately decided to split up. Some of the mutineers, like Peter Heywood, chose to remain in Tahiti and were captured and returned to British justice. Fletcher Christian, who sailed on with the rest of his followers, disappeared into the myths of Pitcairn Island.

Why does such a tale maintain its power even to this day? The amazing story created numerous articles, books and plays when it occurred over 200 years ago, extolling the virtues and evils of Bligh, his men and the cultures involved. Yet even in the 20th century, its allure has barely dimmed as books and films have continued to keep the remarkable legend alive.

The reasons for the mutiny are not hard to appreciate. Unlike most Navy ships of the day, the *Bounty* was too small to accommodate both the space necessary for the transplant of breadfruit and the normal contingent of marines to enforce the orders of the captain. It was left to Bligh and his officers to discipline the men, but Bligh grew increasingly agitated and abusive to his men as officers such as Christian failed to support his command as he saw it. Without the usual assembly of marines to back him up, Bligh was forced to yell, threaten and flog those who, in his eyes, were failing in their duty to their common mission. Subjected to this treatment, Fletcher Christian, shortly after leaving Tahiti for the return voyage and with the memories of the pleasures of that island still fresh in his mind, led a mutiny that has burned an imprint into the Western psyche that continues to intrigue us even to this day. But why?

The Importance of Flow

The ideal, the idea, of paradise is pivotal in the mythology of humankind. Religions everywhere speak of it in some form or other, and it usually encompasses much of what we envision as ease, comfort and joy. In the 18th century, Tahiti came to symbolize this myth in the European mind. This is not idle speculation. Bligh himself felt that the mutiny was largely due to his men's attachment to the women of Tahiti and the fact that they could sustain themselves with a fraction of the effort it took to be a seaman. He wrote in his *Narrative of the Mutiny*:

"...I can only conjecture that they have Idealy assured themselves of a more happy life among the Otaheitians than they could possibly have in England, which joined to some Female connections has most likely been the leading cause of the whole business..."

And later in the same passage he continues:

"...what a temptation it is to such wretches when they find it in their power however illegally it can be got at, to fix themselves in the most of plenty in the finest Island in the World where they need not labour, and where the allurements of dissipation are more than equal to anything that can be conceived."

Paradise had been found. Why leave it?

We can easily appreciate the biological sense of this. I remember listening to a science program on the radio comparing the bones of Neanderthals to Homo sapiens of the same period. Researchers noted that the bones of Neanderthals were larger than their human counterparts, indicating that Neanderthals had been the physically stronger species. So why did they die out?

They were stronger specifically because they were dumber. The study emphasized that one of the keys to evolutionary survival was the conservation of energy. Homo sapiens had smaller muscles because they were smarter at figuring out how to live with less effort, not more. They figured out more efficient ways to conserve energy and survive, and had the smaller muscles to prove it.

Both Tahitians and Europeans were obviously members of the same species, but that's about where the similarities ended. Simply stated, Tahitians in the 18th century were far healthier and it took far less effort for them to maintain that state of health relative to their European counterparts. Tahitians were physically in much better shape than their British visitors. There were tall, well muscled and had good teeth due to their climate, diet and lifestyle. The British were so enamored of their physical appearance that they took a few Tahitians back to England to present to their king. Although, after some initial conflict, they welcomed Europeans, what the Tahitians thought of the British sailors' sickly appearance and smell after months at sea without bathing can only be surmised. It is assumed that they took them to a stream before they took them to bed.

And the degree of physical openness and generosity the Tahitians displayed toward the British had a definite counterpart in their emotional openness, as well. The environment and culture of Tahitian life made them open and expansive in a way that stunned their European visitors. The *Bounty* was in Tahiti for over five months, the longest period of interaction between Tahitians and Europeans to that time. Tahitian families adopted British sailors for the duration of their stay. The Tahitians could empathize with the sufferings of a flogged British sailor to the extent that they would actually wail and scrape their skulls with sharp shells, bleeding profusely, at the sight of one their adopted British family members enduring pain. Can you imagine that response from a Western conqueror over the sufferings of a native?

In Oriental medicine, the idea of flow is central to its theory and application for it is the constriction of energy that ultimately causes disease and sickness, while the open flow of energy through the body's channels creates health and well-being. And we all instinctively know and can feel the difference between this flow and its painful opposite, constriction. It's as evident as the difference between the joy of a vigorous swim in the ocean and the agony of a migraine headache. It's as obvious as the difference between the contentment of full stomach and the pain of an empty one. And it's as clear as the difference between a healthy relationship and one marred by dysfunction. Simply put, flow feels good, and the body is driven by biological evolution to seek this flow and avoid its opposite. It's as natural as the sun rising in the morning.

So the capacity for energetic exchange, for flow, on both a physical and emotional level that was nurtured in the climate and culture of Tahiti was so compelling, so alluring, so tempting, that the men of the *Bounty* risked all to hold onto it. They were driven not only by the undeniable physiological impulses that are part of any being's evolutionary inheritance, but also by the comparison of Tahiti to the harsh life of the sea they knew they would face on the *Bounty* with William Bligh.

The Importance of Balance

But the utopia, the fantasy, of Tahiti was ephemeral for the mutineers of the *Bounty*. They'd had enough of naval discipline and sent Bligh over the side. But then their pendulum swung too far in the opposite direction. Without discipline and coordination, their party turned to drunkenness and infighting, and within a decade all but one were dead, mostly by homicide.

Traumatized and on the verge of extinction from violence and loss of men, the small band left on Pitcairn Island turned to a very strict observance of traditional Christian rituals, ethics and morals. In his monastery, Master Ummon challenged his monks with the question, "The world is vast and wide. Why do you put on your seven-piece robe at the sound of the bell?" And just like that monastery, the residents of Pitcairn Island, though alone in the vast reaches of the Pacific, now signaled the daily activities of their lives, rising, working, playing, eating and relaxing by the sound of a bell. They felt that, in order to survive, they had to put the pendulum back to where it was - no more drunkenness and promiscuity. It was a veritable Jamestown in the South Pacific, with Tahitian women, half-breed children and one surviving mutineer as spiritual leader and patriarch. Interestingly enough, he was a reformed criminal and alcoholic and must have done some fancy footwork to be the only adult male survivor.

It's a sad fact that we often swing from one extreme to the next, unable to find a happy balance. Exaggerated suppression of natural instinct as well as over-indulgence in its impulses are both causes of suffering. But we do not need to repress our own instincts according to the *Book of Job* any more than we need to exaggerate them according to the Book of Hugh Hefner.

In actuality, our lives are filled with plenty, indeed bountiful with the very wisdom of the cosmos. When we're hungry, we eat. When we're tired we sleep. We as humans are able to ponder the mysteries of life. We are the result of the refinement of the matter and energy of the cosmos, of the wisdom of life's flow through almost 14 billion years of time. It is an unmatched miracle. Just the fact that you can read this page and consider it, judge it, for better or worse, is a truth worthy of awe.

When balance is lost, mutinies arise as an unavoidable consequence. If we are to be something other than complete pawns in this game of life, if we are to have any effect, refining the energies we are born with is essential. If the wisdom of these desires and emotions is to be refined, we must see through the delusions that hide them behind a façade of conditioning, inside a cell of intellectual fabrication. For example, men motivated by the belief that sexual energy is bad have actually castrated themselves, but those who operate from a belief that these instinctual energies should be indulged often just create suffering of a different kind. Suffering on both a personal and social level is still the result.

As I said in a previous chapter, we use fire to cook our food, but it's the same fire that burns down the forest. In one sense we call it good, and in the other, bad, but it's the same fire and is not impressed by what we call it. Desire can cause suffering, but the suppression of desire can cause suffering as well. In the end, it is ignorance and delusion that are at the core of much of human suffering. Saints aren't holy. Saints are smart.

Without realization of our True Nature and a commitment to appreciate and balance the energies of our biological existence, we tend to swing from suppression to excess and back again. Refinement of the energies of our lives is impossible if we hold to mythologies about what we should be instead of appreciating what we are. And sadly, the *Bounty*'s mutiny occurs again and again, with nothing to show for it but misery.

The Dharma of Discipline
I've written in this chapter about the importance of flow and its relationship to well-being. But Zen understanding does not reject the limitations imposed by discipline anymore than it chases hastily after a vague notion of flow. They both have their place in life, are ultimately empty and arise naturally according to circumstance.

The cultures of both Tahiti and Britain arose from the long evolutionary march of mankind across the globe in accord with natural laws in differing geographical regions and climates and in response to different social and political challenges. There is no right or wrong here, merely facts. But well-being is not something found only in the South Pacific. The capacity for it exists within each of us, for without this capacity for well-being life would be impossible.

At the beginning of this chapter, I quoted the famous Chinese Zen Master Ummon who said, "The world is vast and wide, why do you put on your seven-piece robe at the sound of the bell?" During the 8th and 9th centuries, Master Ummon led his monks in the disciplined practice of Zen. Traditionally, monks rose well before dawn to meditate, worked in the fields during the day and meditated until late at night. During special training periods, they would commit themselves to meditation for ten to fifteen hours a day, and more, for days, weeks, months and even years. It is not much different in Zen monasteries even today. Although Master Ummon led his monks in a traditional monastic lifestyle that some might view as harsh, their practice of zazen actually promoted well-being to such a degree that many of the famous masters of Zen antiquity lived to be in their 70s and 80s. Ummon himself lived until he was 85, and this in an era when 40 was considered old.

Zen is a disciplined practice and definitely *not* the kind of ease and comfort that attracted the men of the *Bounty* to Tahiti. But well-being is lost, not because we don't live in Tahiti, but because the self-inflicted agitations of the mind constrict the flow of our natural energies and produce an unnecessary doubt, conflict, anxiety and disease. The root of this conflict lies not in harsh climates or even in complex organizations, but in the delusion of a separate and fixed self that we hold deep within our own minds. It is this most basic delusion that conceptually solidifies reality into a plethora of different structures and files, pyramids and coffins. And we expend ourselves in trying to mold the flow of our lives to the golden images we've made. It is an impossible task precisely because our True Nature is vast and boundless. It's like trying to hold the ocean in your hands.

When this delusion of a fixed self and its fixed reality is seen through and allowed to dissolve, there is a real opportunity for an experiential spaciousness that allows our natural energies to flow, calming and energizing our entire being. The monastic practice of Master Ummon and his monks allowed this opportunity to flourish in the practice of zazen and the realization it can produce. This is an example of the true value of discipline.

As human beings in societies, or even as individuals struggling to survive, discipline is an invaluable tool for strength, learning and growth. But a balance between comfort and discipline is required if any goal is to be reached before the effort crumbles under the weight of misguided priorities arising from a slavish adherence to the false gods we can so easily create.

Although even a valuable discipline can often require the suppression of natural tendencies, we can easily pervert its value with misguided priorities. Today many athletes take steroids in order to compete and reach their long cherished dreams of fame and fortune. They are more interested in bolstering their self-image than they are at maintaining the health of their own bodies, the very vehicle of their hoped for success.

I remember as a young boy in school being forced to hold my urine because the bell hadn't rung yet. In boot camp, I recall my drill instructor insisting that I have my "…shit wired tight at all times." We profess to love our children, yet we often accept our own regimentation so unquestioningly that we unconsciously pass along our constricted dysfunction to them.

In doing so, we minimize their own innate organic sense of themselves and help rob them of vitality and joy. We get up at the sound of the alarm clock, we eat when it's time, we punch in and out at work, and we go to bed at a preordained position of Mickey's hands. Our lives are often run neither by biological necessity nor even a valuable discipline. We can easily get stuck in an ant-like maze of existence, unconsciously sacrificed on an altar of incoherent devotion to a job, cause, faith or lifestyle in which we find little solace and the meaning of which we've long forgotten...if we ever knew.

We tend to repeat our mistakes time after time, for our choices can often arise from the knotted ignorance of a conditioned intellect that is only able to direct action from what it knows, and it knows only what it has learned. This particular process of knowing often ignores the signals of the internal organic system that supports it. This is of course not wrong or misguided, but is an invaluable asset in human beings. But it *is* limited. We unconsciously use the conditioned intellect as a veil that covers and silences a deeper pulse of well-being, a voice that can run counter to the dictates of culture and society. This dynamic works to a point, but tends to lead us to a conditioned response inadequate in an ever-changing, flowing and vital world. A famous fighter pilot once said, "There's nothing true in tactics." Like a combat arena where the variables are too vast to comprehend, our lives face challenges that can't easily be addressed by slogans and dictums from the past.

Narrow Beam...Wide Beam

The radars of fighter jets have a very good narrow beam capability. This type of narrow beam radar functions very much like a portable flashlight in that its light beam is rather narrow. It is a requirement in fighter jets because the radar missiles they launch require the kind of signal quality that only fine narrow beam radars can produce.

However, a fighter jet will not enter the combat arena without the guidance of larger wide beam radar provided by either by a ship, AWACS or E-2 early warning aircraft. This radar energy is more like a searchlight in that it can scan large areas and gain a much-needed bigger picture. Fighter pilots need this wide beam guidance to find enemy targets to engage. The narrow beam radar of the fighter jet is like looking through a straw. If you were trying to find a particular star at night while looking through that straw, it would be very difficult. Indeed, a bigger picture would be completely lost to you. Likewise, the straw-like constriction of the fighter radar's narrow beam is not sufficient to get a larger tactical understanding of the unfolding combat arena, or even a positive direction to fly and engage the enemy without the guidance of a wide beam radar.

Both radars emit similar energy that is engineered for different functions, and they are both necessary. The narrow beam capability of fighter jets can identify and engage targets. This identification of and with the target at lock-on is absolutely essential. It is the radar's function and its mission. But it does lack the larger view and is thereby limited. The narrow beam radar naturally locks onto, and identifies with, individual targets out of a myriad of possibilities.

With Zen meditation, the mind's eye naturally dilates. It's like opening wide the lens of a camera to take in a broader view, the same kind of broader view provided by wide beam radars. The wide beam capacity of our mind's eye provides us with the wisdom, understanding and relaxation of the larger picture and releases us from the necessity of locking onto, and of holding to, the separate and individual manifestations that appear in the vast field of possibility. We all have the Eye to realize this innate capacity, but to do so we must abandon the straw of ego that constricts our view. Zen meditation is invaluable for this task.

My favorite symbol for the human ego is the cartoon character Yosemite Sam. He's always mad, always shooting off the pistol that's bigger than he is, always unable to catch that varmint Bugs Bunny. He's so short that his view is constricted. He can only see what's in front of him. He doesn't have the big picture.

You can't see many stars at all while looking at the night sky through a straw. Likewise, for us to get a broader appreciation of life we need to discard the straw and allow our perceptual lens to dilate. Only then can we understand why Bugs Bunny is always laughing.

There is a line from the Diamond Sutra that advises us to, "Arouse the mind without fixing it anywhere." This is the mind of the warrior and in the end, in this life, we are all warriors.

Ummon and Heywood

How are Master Ummon and the Bounty midshipman Peter Heywood related? Master Ummon lived the regimented life of a monastic Zen Master, leading them in a practice designed to help them realize this vast and wide universe as themselves. Without this realization, true well-being becomes more elusive for we are like the deaf, unable to hear and appreciate its voice.

Peter Heywood spent a year and a half on the island of Tahiti before being captured. He married, made friends, enjoyed his Tahitian life and retained the tattoos they gave him throughout his life, hidden skillfully beneath his stiff British uniform. After surviving his trial for mutiny with a King's pardon and being reinstated to the Navy, he had a long and successful career as a British Naval Officer. He wrote:

"And after all is said and done among us great and wise people of the earth, pray what do we all toil for, late take rest, and eat the bread of carefulness, but to reach, at last, the very state to which they are born…ease of circumstances, and the option of being idle or busy as we please? If I go on this way you will say I am a savage, and so I believe I am, and ever shall be in some points…"

These words came from a letter he wrote to a friend near the end of his life and are indicative of a mind still torn by the stark contrast that he had witnessed, that he had lived.

On Tahiti, probably for the first time in his life, he was able to respond to his natural instincts without the regimentation of British sensibilities and allow the warm energetic breezes of his own makeup to balance themselves in harmony with the sun and the tide, with the wind and the sea. The physical and emotional ease and comfort he knew on the island of Tahiti, and its hint of well-being, remained in his memory, hidden like his Tahitian tattoos, unwelcome below the stiff scowl of British discipline. Yet he longed to feel its medicinal embrace once more, like a lover longs for his beloved, like a mystic yearns to be united with God.

Zen Master Ummon asked, "The world is vast and wide, why do you put on your seven-fold robe at the sound of the bell?" He challenged his monks, and he challenges us, asking why we scurry around so, on a timescale relevant neither to natural instinct nor wise discipline, but by one dictated by the cold regimentation of coordination, control or blind repetition.

Though separated by almost a thousand years, Master Ummon and Peter Heywood meet in a place where all beings meet, at the fountain of well-being. It is epitomized by the dynamic of flow, by the vitality of energetic exchange, and is part and parcel of our evolutionary heritage. There is a Buddhist blessing which says:

> May you be filled with loving-kindness
> May you be free from inner and outer danger
> May you be well in body, heart and mind
> May you be peaceful and truly happy.

True well-being exists when the various physical, emotional and mental strands of our lives are balanced and in harmony, and happiness is the result. This, of course, is not just a Buddhist sentiment; human beings in all places and in all times have desired this. Yet in this life it may seem almost impossible, subjected as we all are to the slings and arrows of outrageous fortune. The poor and the sick are handed challenges that can appear insurmountable.

But our challenge is not to generate suffering needlessly. Master Ummon's question to his monks, asking them why they scurried about donning their seven-piece robe at the sound of the bell, may seem perplexing. As master of his temple, he was the one making them do it. Yet he knew, beyond a shadow of a doubt, if his monks could not truly realize themselves *as* this vast and wide universe that they would not escape the endless cycle of suffering that ignorance produces as easily and inevitably as a virus causes sickness. Their practice, rising early and meditating long, was his way of shaking them loose from the cobwebs of their delusion. This is the traditional practice of Zen, and the realization it offers releases the mind from the shackles of its own making, allowing the voice of well-being to be heard more clearly.

Though the effects of societies' demands on individuals exist in any culture where humans gather, from Tahitian villages to large European cities, for a short period of time in the 18th century a meeting between these two vastly different cultures took place. We saw how one small Tahitian society allowed natural instinct to flourish largely unhindered because there was no particular need to thwart it. We saw how British culture was deeply challenged by what it witnessed. The Tahitians did not share the same gods or the same taboos, yet seemed carefree and happy in a way the English could only fantasize about. It haunted Peter Heywood to the end of his days and made him wonder why we great and wise people of the earth struggled so day-to-day, when in the end, we were all savages, natives yearning for a balance and harmony to our lives where peace and happiness had greater possibility, and a chance to flow unhindered by inordinate constriction.

The hint of well-being that haunted Peter Heywood can disappear as quickly as the paradise of Tahiti did after being subjected to European influence. Well-being cannot exist in isolation. Its physical, mental and emotional energies intertwine like vines around a tree. There is no fixed state of well-being. It flows like the wind and surges like the tide. If we can let go of the static nature of the intellectual distortion that hides it behind a wall of accumulated knowledge and conditioning, we can better hear the delicate voice of well-being as it offers its wisdom, subtle yet constant. Listening deeply to this subtle vibration, we can make better choices. We can move toward a fuller appreciation of well-being for ourselves and others. It is a practice, and it's endless. This is one of the great values of Zen.

Religions arouse in human cultures because we felt the loss of connection with something profound. Call it Nature, call it Soul, call it Emptiness, call it God, call it whatever you like. When we realize our True Nature and the connection is made, all words melt and become meaningless…meaningless in the light, like a fog receding from the sun. The potential for well-being is a child of this light.

Chapter Nine

SWORDFIGHTING AND AIR COMBAT
(and maybe some sports to warm up)
The Importance of Zen in Action

"Zen practice pursued within activity is a million times superior to that pursued within tranquility."
—Master Hakuin (1689-1769 CE)

It's one thing to meditate in your cave or on your cushion and realize the true nature, the empty nature, of existence. It is indeed a wonderful thing and has far reaching consequences. But what about when we stand up and begin to move and flow within a multitude of variables and influences? Is the tranquility and focus of meditation soon lost? Indeed, is there any need to hold on to it? These questions go straight to the heart of not only what meditation really means, but also to its practical application in daily life.

The title of this chapter, *Swordfighting and Air Combat*, is provocative and is a touchy subject in modern American Zen. Although there is very little pacifism in the Japanese Zen we have inherited, the pacifist influence in American Zen is substantial and led by some notable teachers.

I will address the philosophical and political implications of the use of violence as it relates to Zen understanding and compassion in the next chapter. For now, I feel it is important to first talk of the practical application of meditation and understanding as it applies not only to fighting, but to more peaceful pursuits as well.

Let's Have Fun!

We don't need to go to war to get a handle on the practical application of meditation in action. We do it all the time, albeit unconsciously perhaps. Almost anything that we find appealing draws us into a natural focus: a work of art, a beautiful person, an interesting story or a challenging activity. Although there are many ways to meditate, virtually all methods produce a single pointed focus that merges the perceiver and the perceived into an experiential, unified whole where dualistic stereotypes dissolve in the reality of the moment. In Zen, this is called *samadhi*. The practice of *shikantaza*, a Soto Zen method which is often described as panoramic, choiceless awareness, uses samadhi to let go of whatever sensation, idea, fantasy or daydream that may arise so that the meditator may emerge onto the wide, open plain of pure awareness without any specific object of meditation. The point is this: meditation, like any activity we find appealing, draws us out of our heads. It releases us from the stories that run constantly in our minds, like a scratched record that plays over and over. And although we like to believe that we control our minds and our ideas, these explanations of how things are actually run *us*, sometimes into the ground. This is why we like our entertainments, our hobbies, even our drugs…for they give us some respite from all that tiresome noise.

…Catch a Wave and You're Sittin' on Top of the World…. The Beach Boys

A young Tibetan Lama named Kinley went to Colorado to study, and during his summer vacation went to Hawaii and surfed for the first time. His comments on that occasion are quite revealing. When he first saw the ocean, it made him so relaxed. He was honest and admitted a lot of stress involved in the culture shock of study in America. But all the stress in his mind disappeared immediately upon seeing the ocean. He'd heard about the calming power of the ocean and he found it to be true.

When we meditate, our whole metabolism slows an average of twenty percent in the stillness of motion and slowed pace of breathing. He said he preferred the slow pace of his home country, and that the ocean gave him that same feeling of slowness. When he surfed and was finally able to stand up, that gliding feeling made him totally present in the moment. He reflected on how we are usually distracted, and that distraction was the greatest obstacle to meditation. But when he was surfing and gliding on the waves he was totally present, naturally, without effort.

Human beings naturally separate their experience into inner and outer realms. We normally appreciate that our thoughts, for example, take place inside of us, and that our brain and nervous systems process information from outside of us. This is not an inaccurate view, of course, but it is limiting. Human beings possess the capability to perceive and appreciate a non-dual oneness of perception that transcends and informs this narrow and more limited view.

The oneness experienced in meditation, in samadhi, is a very natural state, not something bizarre or abnormal. Even those who do not meditate flow into and out of these states all the time. It's merely a matter of concentration and focus on what is normally considered the outside world, where our normal ego chatter is silenced by the beauty, awe or compelling nature of the activity in which we are engaged.

Of course, there are levels of meditation beyond these active states. Serious practitioners may have access to levels where not only has the self disappeared in intense focus on the object of meditation, but the object itself disappears in the absorption of deep meditation. Master Rinzai talked about these various states in his Four Propositions.

1. *Sometimes you take away the man without taking away the object.*
This is the active meditation we've just discussed, like Lama Kinley's wave riding, total presence in the activity of surfing.

2. *Sometimes you take away the object without taking away the man.*
This is a state of consciousness familiar to everyone where the self, or ego, is fully engrossed inward upon itself.

3. *Sometimes you take away both the object and the man.*
This is the deep absorption of meditation mentioned above, where the practitioner is neither conscious of self nor object, but is not asleep, either.

4. *Sometimes you take away neither the object nor the man.*
This is a very normal state of consciousness where we run back and forth from perception of the external world to an internal comment or judgment about it.

These Four Propositions of Master Rinzai are the ways in which he sees our consciousness functioning. Propositions Numbers 2 and 4 are very familiar to us. Proposition Number 3 is familiar to those serious practitioners of meditation. But Proposition Number 1 is an active meditation that we all participate in from time to time, but may not appreciate fully. We do it when we make love, when we play and when we create. It is a natural form of samadhi.

Golf is Life

Beyond the positive effects of meditative focus that naturally occurs from compelling activity, we actually learn many of the same lessons that spiritual practice teaches when we approach the joyful tests of sport with a mind willing to learn.

Lama Kunga Rinpoche, a Tibetan Buddhist teacher sent to the West by the Dalai Lama, is an avid golfer, hacking away on California fairways in his monk's robes. He said, "…the origins of suffering come from anger, frustration, self-consciousness. If you play golf, you know what I mean."

Anyone who has ever played the game can see how easily the ego steps in to impede desired results. In this sense, an uncontrolled desire to get what we want actually gets in the way of getting what we want. It's a conundrum. If I didn't have a desire to hit the ball long, or at least straight, I wouldn't be there to begin with. But that very desire, if unrefined through practice, actually causes the body to tense up. Tight muscles are slow muscles. The result is an endless stream of poor shots, interspersed with the customary foul language. Golf is a four-letter word!

Lama Kunga feels that golf is 90% physical. He likes his mental attitude toward the game but feels that starting late in life hurt him. He wants to be reincarnated as a better golfer. And I think he's right. The highest levels of golf require not only a refined and focused mind but also an agile, coordinated body as well.

However, the spiritual lessons can be learned even with a high handicap. The famous golfer Ben Hogan once said that, in a round of golf, he would hit only four or five good shots, but that the rest were manageable. Of course, a good shot for Ben Hogan and a good shot for me would be two different things entirely. But just imagine: one of the greatest golfers who ever lived felt he only hit four or five good shots in a round of golf, out of almost 70 total shots! It's not how good your good shots are that counts, it's how good your bad shots are. That's the essence of refinement. It's not about being brilliant all the time. It's about limiting your mistakes, and learning from the ones you make; being grateful for the lessons learned instead of anguishing foolishly over not achieving some unrealistic standard that exists only in fantasy. The greatest golfer of all time, Bobby Jones, said, "The object of golf is to beat someone. Make sure that someone is not yourself."

Can we not see how we do this to ourselves in daily life? How often do we beat ourselves up over honest mistakes, over being human? This only impedes the game. Crying over spilt milk, as it were, merely sets us up to spill the next glass, for the agitated mind tightens us just at a time when the game requires awareness and flow. That game is Life. We can't play it very well if we bind ourselves through unrealistic identification with stories concocted by Madison Avenue. Let's face it. I AM NOT TIGER WOODS! Beyond that, I am not Jesus Christ, I am not Bill Gates, I am not Gandhi, Mother Theresa or anyone else excellent, prominent or well-known. But I'm having one helluva good time. I'm captivated by seeing and learning about this miraculous breath we call Life.

Shunryu Suzuki Roshi, one of the seminal figures of Zen in the West, defined zazen meditation as merely sitting down, and getting out of the way. Even spiritual aspiration must be abandoned in the end if there is to be any realization. Likewise, any athlete comes to his or her sport with a great desire to succeed. But when the actual game begins, that very desire must be abandoned in order for success to happen.

In zazen, for example, posture is of primary importance. It takes a certain amount of practice to learn and integrate the technical aspects of sitting so that the physical posture becomes largely automatic and unconscious. Likewise, most sporting activities require a good deal of practice to achieve the physical movements necessary for the task at hand. An even greater effort is required to achieve a naturalness and unconscious ability to perform the tasks so that the mind can focus on the goal without wasting energy in concentration on the physical mechanics. Because seated meditation is mostly static in nature, this is rather direct and uncomplicated.

However, it is quite the opposite in golf and other sports. But once a certain amount of physical dexterity is achieved, there still remains the mental aspect to be appreciated. In golf, as in meditation, the ego must rest and allow a natural flow to occur. The constriction that the overactive ego naturally produces inhibits the flow of the swing, as it inhibits the flow of energy that the mind/body produces as effortlessly as the lungs breathe, or the wind blows. It is this very constriction that inhibits progress.

Swordfighting and Air Combat

Let's escalate the discussion to include fighting. As I mentioned earlier, the subject of fighting and its obvious violence is a hot topic in American Zen. I will cover these important issues in the next chapter, but first let's see some of the history behind it.

The most prominent figure in this regard is Master Takuan. Born in 1573, this Zen Master lived through the most tumultuous period in Japan's history where the country was torn apart by competing warlords. This warring period finally gave birth to the Tokugawa Shogunate that unified and pacified the country. He was literally a child of this conflict that broiled unchecked during his youth and ended with the decisive battle of Sekigahara in 1600. For Master Takuan, unshielded by any distance from the conflict that is the luxury of many critics, violence was just a fact of life.

Even so, he lived the life of a monk and, at age 37, was made abbot of Daitoku-ji, one of the main monasteries of the Rinzai sect. He fell out of favor with the second shogun, Hidetada, and was banished for a time. However, the third shogun, Iemitsu, admired Takuan and built a temple in Edo (Tokyo) for him, Tokai-ji. There he lived until his death in 1645. He taught Zen to the famous samurai, Yagyu Munemori, who himself was the instructor of swordsmanship to the first three Tokugawa shoguns.

In the last chapter, I pointed out the famous line in the Diamond Sutra that advises us to, "…arouse the mind without fixing it anywhere." As I stated, this is the mind of the warrior and is the essence of Takuan's teaching in regard to swordfighting, or kendo, the Way of the Sword. In one of his writings, *The Record of Divine Immovable Intelligence*, he writes:

"Fudo means not to move, but not as a lifeless stone or tree. Fudochi, immovable wisdom, means to move here and there, right and left, in every direction wherever the mind wants to, without its stopping on and clutching any one object….When you are going to be struck by an enemy's sword, if you put your mind on it, your activity is thwarted and you will be killed by him….If you do not attach your mind to the sword or its movement or some plan or theory of fighting, you can turn the opponent's sword in his direction and kill him."

Master Takuan takes for granted that the physical skills and internal courage required for swordfighting are already present. All that is left to do is to train and refine the mind's energy in accordance with the activity. Inordinate fear is a distraction, but controlled fear can be helpful, as in the example of night carrier landings I discussed earlier in the book. Anger, rage and impetuous desire to win are also obstacles for, as in golf, they tighten the body just at a time when speed, fluidity and agile responsiveness are required.

This can be further clarified by looking at the art of air combat, or dogfighting, as it is popularly known. Dogfighting, like the art of kendo, is a dying skill, a dying art, and its lifespan will be much shorter than that of kendo due to the advancing technology of unpiloted drones.

Modern day fighter pilots live in perhaps the most exciting, dynamic and demanding environment that ever existed, with speeds, accelerations, altitudes and forces of gravity that most men cannot even imagine, a command of time and space that cannot be fathomed by normal human beings. What the Red Baron and other heralded fighter pilots of the First World War experienced was very different from today's air combat arena. In those days, in order to get shot down, the enemy had to be close enough to kiss you. The speeds were so slow and the diameters of turning fights so small that keeping sight of the enemy was relatively simple. Not much different in the Second World War, either.

But since Vietnam, it has been a completely different story. With the closure rates of modern supersonic fighters, an enemy ten miles away can be met in 30 seconds. The diameter of a turning fight can reach out to four miles and maintaining sight of the enemy, a crucial factor in a dogfight, becomes a major problem. Lost sight, lost fight, they say. Likewise, air-to-air missiles can be launched from miles away, beyond visual range in the case of radar guided missiles.

Everything can happen so fast. If you merge with enemy jets with a poor awareness of their actual numbers and locations, you can be dead before you blink. The technology has exceeded the level of awareness that the human mind is capable of handling, unable to filter and respond in time. Being a fighter pilot requires the acrobatic sense of a gymnast, the instincts of a tiger, and the calm, concentrative awareness of a recluse able to filter through all the screaming confusion and react under the relentless pounding pressure of high 'G' forces and surging adrenaline.

This occurred in a profession that was born in the 20th century, but will not outlive the 21st. For a mere speck of recorded time, men take airplanes into the air and fight in them. For a hundred years of human experience, a chosen few, the keenest among us, tumble in the skies with one another in a world that none before or after would ever know.

I feel truly privileged to have been a part of it. I practiced air combat, dogfighting, for 15 years in the U.S. Navy, was a graduate of Topgun and flew as an adversary instructor pilot. That means, in addition to flying F-14 Tomcats, I also flew Soviet Mig simulating aircraft as an enemy adversary pilot training our fleet to meet the Soviet threat of that day as was depicted in the Tom Cruise film, *Topgun*. I also gave the "One vs. One Dogfight" lecture to several squadrons in the Pacific Fleet for a time in our Air Combat Readiness Training program. Over the many years that I had the privilege to fight against the fine pilots of the U.S. Navy, I began to appreciate just what Master Takuan was teaching.

In the most basic dogfight training we have, two pilots will face off in the same type of jet, i.e., two F-14s will engage in a training dogfight. This is called One vs. One Similar, because the jets are the same. It is the best teacher of pilot skill because, with both jets being of equal performance capability, the only variable is the pilot.

The famous golfer Jack Nicklaus once said, "A lot of times you don't actually win so much as the other guys lose." This is precisely how I felt about dogfighting. When jets of equal performance pass nose to nose at the same altitude and speed, at that point the sum of all forces is zero. Nothing can be gained, and nothing can be lost. Unless, of course, you insist upon it.

In my later years as a fighter pilot, I felt that all I had to do was maneuver my jet at maximum performance. This was not that difficult. Even a relatively inexperienced pilot could do that. After that, all I did was open my mind's eye, my awareness, and look at my opponent without fear or hate, and without undue desire to win. I merely followed the dictum of Gichin Funakoshi, the father of modern karate, who said, "Don't be anxious to win. But be very determined not to lose." This is a fine line, but an important one. As stated previously, an exaggerated aggressiveness leads to mistakes, mistakes that arise from an inability to appreciate that in this scenario the sum of all forces is zero and you can neither win nor lose, unless an opening is provided. This opening is usually made not by the pilot who is unskilled really, but by the pilot who doesn't understand the truth of this scenario.

Exaggerated aggressive maneuvers to win, to beat the opponent, open gaps, cracks in the geometrical structure of the fight where initially none existed. A scenario where the sum of all forces is zero is like a perfect circle, a seamless whole. A skilled pilot who flies with a wide-open awareness will naturally maneuver his jet into the gaps left by an overly aggressive opponent and gain an advantageous firing position with little or no self-conscious effort. Here, determination to win means little, but awareness is like a high-pressure system which flows easily and naturally into an area of lower pressure. A tense mind, whether fearful or bloodthirsty, is weakened and made brittle by its own agitation.

One of the last great samurai was a man named Yamaoka Tesshu (1836-1888). He was also a serious lay Zen student who was enlightened under Tekisui Giboku Roshi and received dharma transmission from him. He was considered one of the top two swordsmen in Japan at the time. Tesshu and the other famous swordsman once met in a duel. It was a training duel with bamboo swords in a dojo packed with students eager to finally witness the duel of the century. Nothing happened. The sword masters stood facing each other, bamboo swords at the ready position, for a full 45 minutes before each slowly backed away and bowed, ending the duel.

How perfect! They both realized that with equal skills and equal weapons there really was nothing to gain. The only contest was mental. But here one refined awareness met another, like two high-pressure systems leaning against each other. No agitation, no fear, no blood lust. Just pure awareness. Therefore there were no gaps, no cracks in the dynamic encounter. There was nothing to do but leave.

The practice of meditation, of Zen, has a wide array of practical applications that are of course not limited to sports and fighting. It's a practice that can illumine any human endeavor, for, wherever man goes, in the end he must always face the challenge of his worst enemy: his own mind. Unlike a Hollywood movie where the hero becomes a master in two hours and rides into the sunset finally complete, the real practice is endless, simply because life has no beginning and no end. The sword master Yagyu Munemori said:

"...there is a superior stage, in the way of swordsmanship. When you go deep into the way, you realize there are no limits in the end. There is no point where you can say this is it, and you see starkly how inadequate you are. So you spend the rest of your life without even thinking of becoming accomplished or without thinking of boasting, let alone looking down upon others."

The famous golfer Tiger Woods echoed these same sentiments when he said in an interview, "You're never there. You'll never get there. But it sure is fun trying."

But Yagyu Munemori did accomplish one great feat that is shown in this statement from his later years. "I have yet to learn how to win a fight with others, but I have learned to win a fight with myself."

Chapter Ten

THE DELUSION OF APPEARANCES
The Importance of Compassion in the Realm of Violence

> Thus shall ye think of all this fleeting world;
> A star at dawn, a bubble in a stream;
> A flash of lightning in a summer cloud,
> A flickering lamp, a phantom, and a dream.
> —A stanza from the Diamond Sutra

September 11

I know I'll always wonder whether my friend from the Navy, Tom McGuinness, was still alive or even conscious when the plane he was co-piloting slammed into the World Trade Center on September 11, 2001. His plane, American Airlines Flight 11, was the first plane to go down that awful day, a day that has surely changed the course of history.

It was hard to pull myself away from the television, sitting as I was in stupefied horror as they replayed the event over and over. If asked how I felt, the only image that comes to mind is of the poster therapists have on their walls these days ... the one with all the faces on them: the sad faces, shocked faces, depressed, fearful, mad, angry faces. If you take all the bad ones, roll them up into one big ball and multiply it by ten, that's about how I felt. I really couldn't pull one feeling from another as they seemed to roll from one to the other and back again at random, so fast that they were indistinguishable. Just one big blob of fearful, angry dread. Transmigrating through the hell realms, big time.

The next few days were even worse. I was determined to get back on the horse and flew my regularly scheduled trip to Honolulu. Many pilots were calling in refusing to fly, and flight attendants were actually quitting their jobs. We keep a crash axe in the cockpit for an emergency breakout, and my captain actually kept it by his seat, determined to whack any intruder. Such was the atmosphere so soon after the attack.

Yet it was a gorgeous day in the islands, one of the best in recent memory, and I couldn't enjoy it in the least. Sitting on my surfboard in the pristine waters of Ala Moana, near Waikiki, a sublime rejuvenating tropical sunrise did absolutely nothing to ease the pain. In the midst of paradise, life did nothing but suck.

It was then that I began to look into how my Zen practice helped me deal with this dilemma, or didn't. How was Zen equipped to ease the suffering of its adherents as other religions attempted to ease the suffering of theirs?

9/11 genuinely focuses this discussion of compassion and violence. We, at home, cannot hide from the modern realities of conflict. We cannot send our armies to deal with unpleasant realities far away while we sit at home, safe in our castles of certainty, comfortable in our judgments and our condemnations. The enemy in this war is here and can strike at any time. 9/11 has given us the opportunity to really examine our truths, our judgments, our compassion and our violence.

In the last chapter, we discussed some of the practical applications of Zen practice and understanding. We saw how they could be applied to the modest activities of modern sports and also how they have been traditionally incorporated in the samurai art of kendo, or swordfighting. We also looked at how that ancient pursuit is still relevant today in modern air combat.

But I really don't want to leave anyone with the impression that Zen is merely another avenue for success. Although I can speak about the practical application of Zen practice, to be honest, I'm not that interested in Zen as an avenue toward greater accomplishments in sports, war or individual endeavors. All that is really just a sideshow. The deeper value of Zen lies in its ability to satisfy the persistent deep-seated doubt of humankind, a doubt that has caused unnecessary grief since the dawn of consciousness itself.

In conjunction with the resolution of doubt, traditional Zen also emphasizes that the flip side of this wisdom is compassion. Wisdom dissolves doubt and compassion naturally flows forth. So the question is…where is it? Where is compassion in all this talk of the power of mental equanimity and awareness amidst the ego-cultivated stress of competition and war?

The wisdom of compassion is expressed in the observation of the precepts. As Maezumi Roshi once told me, "If you understand the precepts, you understand Zen. They are not two different things." Because of my military background, I am often asked how I reconcile my former occupation with the first precept of Buddhism, non-killing. In our sect, it is taken as a vow, i.e., I vow to appreciate and affirm all life and not kill. In our practice of Zen, we deal with the precepts as koans, and we do it at the very end of formal koan study. A student may study from 10 to 20 years before finally dealing with the precepts in a very deep and intimate way with his or her teacher.

In Zen, we address the precepts from three different angles, known as Hinayana, Mahayana and Buddhayana. Of course, the terms Hinayana and Mahayana denote the two main sects of Buddhism in Asia, with Zen being an offshoot of Mahayana Buddhism. But as a means to address the precepts, we use the terms to focus on three main aspects. Simply put, the Hinayana approach takes the precepts literally and fundamentally. If it says don't kill, then don't kill, period.

The Mahayana approach is broader and tries to take into account right time, right person, right place and right amount. It might be described by some as situational ethics; that is, what is compassionate action at a given time depends on a number of variables, not all of which, perhaps, can be clearly known.

The final aspect, Buddhayana, addresses the Absolute view that Life is One and Undivided from the beginning, and in the case of the first precept non-killing, emphasizes the point that originally there is *no one to kill*, and *no one to do the killing*.

We study these three aspects of the precepts in depth at the very end of formal study because it is vitally important to have an appreciation of the whole teaching of Zen in order to clearly see the value of all three and be able to flow easily between them.

We can look at these three different aspects, the Hinayana, Mahayana and Buddhayana, from the perspective of differing apertures of perception. Sometimes, due to our close proximity to an event or issue, it is important to narrow our focus and simply follow the rules as written. We can see that, in certain circumstances, there is no room for maneuver or time for evaluation. Immediate action is called for, and our best approximation of what might be appropriate may be found in strict adherence to a code or set of rules, like monks in a monastery, or soldiers on a battlefield. This is akin to a Hinayana approach.

Likewise, our human consciousness is normally limited to a habitual narrow focus where what is termed self-consciousness, or ego-consciousness, predominates in the seat of perception. This mode of perception is narrow and its conditioned commentary, judging the distillates of sense perception, is continuous. Often this narrow view takes itself and its judgments as the only reality it can rely on, and a fixed code or set of rules may be the only skillful means of right conduct that it may understand and follow at a particular time.

But all human beings are endowed with greater capacity than this. With spiritual practice, human beings are able to widen their perceptual apparatus and appreciate life without ego-consciousness dominating the seat of perception. With this broader vision the ego is merely another voice in a vast plain of perceptive possibility, and we are better able to gain a more balanced view. If we are better able to take in a broader view, we can gain a better understanding of the causal factors of any particular situation. A general viewing a battlefield through the wide lens of his binoculars may be able to see that he is losing on a particular front, not for the lack of courage of his men but merely by unavoidable realities that are not the fault of those fighting. This clarity, not shared by his men at the front, gives him the ability to choose different options and better engage his other forces.

Likewise, animals in a jungle live an eat-or-be-eaten existence. But scientists studying them from a broader perspective can appreciate something much greater. Plants give animals the oxygen needed for life while animals breathe out the carbon dioxide and excrete the dung, or fertilizer, that plants need for their existence. Plant-eating animals, herbivores, at a minimum, are necessary for the carbon dioxide and fertilizer to be present for the plants. Carnivores help keep the herbivores in check so that the plant life and animal life, the flora and fauna of our planet, can maintain the balance necessary for life to flourish.

Scientific knowledge allows a broader perspective of this jungle and affords us a peace and contentment in the understanding that the seeming violence of the narrower view actually contributes to a larger balance that is absolutely necessary for the jungle to exist at all, and for us to exist to appreciate its marvelous functioning. Like lions that are sometimes engaged in ferocious combat, and sometimes atop a high rock viewing the Serengeti plain in all its splendor, we, too, are engaged not only with the challenges of life and the narrow but necessary views it can produce, but we are also blessed with a mind that is vast and can appreciate the wide panorama of knowledge and understanding that comes with it. This is an understanding akin to the Mahayana approach to the precepts.

My wife often uses the analogy of a pregnant woman being rushed to a hospital by her anxious husband. A policeman, following a strict Hinayana approach, would pull them over to write a speeding ticket. But once aware of the actual circumstances, he would turn on his siren and lead them through every red light possible to get them to the hospital safely. Here the policeman's understanding of the larger situation would enable him to take a compassionate action that is appropriate. This is the functioning of the Mahayana approach to the precepts.

Finally, the Buddhayana view is the most spacious of all, and arises from the very realization and enlightenment of Buddhist practice. As stated previously, in the case of the first precept, there is no one to kill and no one to do the killing. As the Patriarch Bodhidharma said, "In vast emptiness, there is nothing holy." This view is so vast that the term loses its meaning, for there is no boundary anywhere that determines its limit. And concurrently the perception is so sharp that it penetrates the cloaking device of logic and glimpses the permeable and empty nature of the flow of all existence. Realizing this we can truly rest, even amidst the trials and travails of life. This perspective of oneself and the cosmos as One, empty and eternal, is marked by an appreciation of the unmatched beauty, harmony and balance of an existence which is whole and complete precisely because it is inherently empty, transparent and without the distinctions of space, time or individual identity. It is the broadest view of which we speak, and requires true realization, or enlightenment, to appreciate fully.

Compassion in the Realm of Violence

The question to me remains: how do I reconcile my former job as a fighter pilot with the first precept of Buddhism? I do it in the following way with a thought experiment, and this approach would fall into the second category of dealing with the precepts, the Mahayana aspect. What is compassion in the realm of violence? Many people feel that compassion and violence are at all times incompatible, that one energy cannot co-exist with the other. But is that true?

Let's say I'm at home with my family and an intruder armed with a knife bursts through the door, screaming madly and heads for my wife or child. Let's also imagine that I happen to have a weapon, a gun, available. What do I do? What should I do? I don't have time to reason with the deranged man. I have but a spilt second to act, or not. If I shoot him, I may indeed kill him. If I don't shoot him, he may kill an innocent person, a loved one. At that moment, where is my compassion?

I am an airline pilot. If I had the means at my disposal, would I refrain from killing a terrorist and thereby allow my plane to be used as a weapon resulting in the deaths of hundreds, even thousands, in the air and on the ground? Where is my compassion then?

Frankly, I would shoot an intruder or a terrorist. In my view, my compassionate responsibility lies first with my family and those I'm charged to protect. I don't know what karmic interactions led the intruder to my house or the terrorist to my airplane, but with all due respect to their humanity, they are going to need another rebirth to get it right. Where do my responsibility and my compassion end? What if my neighbor's child were similarly threatened? What about the guy down the street and his family? Where do my responsibility and my compassion end? At the corner? At the state line? At the country's border? At the cockpit door?

I asked this question to a noted pacifist of our sect. He admitted that he was not sure what he would actually do in the moment, but that he hoped he would not act in a way harmful to anyone, even the intruder. He felt that violence never solved anything, and that any violence was merely a continuation of man's delusion. He would not act violently to save himself or anyone dear to him. Such was his philosophy, an approach more in line with the Hinayana view.

I have deep respect for this monk, for as a Vietnam veteran he has his own experience to speak from. He speaks from firsthand knowledge about the horrible consequences of violence and a deep commitment to the Buddha Way. He knows very clearly what many do not. He knows, even without the use of physical violence at all, how harmful our anger and hatred is to ourselves and our own happiness, how it poisons our own well more than it actually harms those we might despise.

Sadly, violence does solve things. After the Third Punic War when Rome finally defeated Carthage, the city was completely destroyed and the land was sowed with salt so that nothing would ever grow. Rome had no further problems with Carthage. But it's also true that their use of violence as a primary foreign policy had its eventual backlash as at least a partial causal factor in the fall of their own empire. Such was the way of the world, and probably still is.

At best, violence may be only a short-term solution. That's true. But a short-term solution may be the only solution that is viable at the time. If a person allows himself or herself to be harmed, even killed, by another without defending themselves because that defense may cause harm to the attacker, that is their choice. But could we honestly say that it is a moral choice to not act at all, ever, even in defense of the innocent? Likewise, if we say that in extreme cases the use of violence may be justified, even moral, then haven't we just shifted the discussion from a moral to a political one? Isn't the argument now not if we should use violence, but when, where and against whom? My last teacher, Tenshin Roshi, says that it's obvious we didn't get to the top of the food chain by being nice. What is important now is how we deal with that aspect of our nature in a constructive way.

This truly is a koan with no easy answer. What leads us into such traps, such necessity of choosing between horrifying alternatives? Again, Zen would insist it is the delusion of the human mind, a mind that insists on turning impermanent ideas into eternal truths, relative names into absolute gods, and social conventions into commandments and inquisitions, a dysfunctional quest that ultimately sacrifices our breath, our beauty and our very lives on a foolish altar of hypocrisy.

The Delusion of Appearances

I began this chapter with a quote from the Diamond Sutra entitled the Delusion of Appearances:

> "Thus shall ye think of all this fleeting world:
> A star at dawn, a bubble in a stream;
> A flash of lightning in a summer cloud,
> A flickering lamp, a phantom, and a dream."

This Diamond Sutra was composed in India around the fourth century CE. A Chinese copy dated to 868 CE is the oldest extant printed book in the world, predating Beowulf by several hundred years. It is highly revered in the Mahayana tradition, especially in Zen.

A very similar sentiment is expressed in the marvelous poem which springs from the Islamic world, The Rubaiyat of Omar Khayam.

> "For in and out, above, about, below,
> 'Tis nothing but a Magic Shadow-show
> Play'd in a Box whose Candle is the Sun,
> Round which we Phantom Figures come and go."

We in the West are not devoid of this sentiment. We are not ignorant of this feeling, this realization. William Blake wrote:

> "We are led to believe a lie
> When we see not thro' the eye.
> Which was born in a night to perish in a night
> When the soul slept in beams of light."

Every tradition of mankind speaks, at some point, of this truth. Buddhism describes it as the illusory nature of reality and teaches of the dangers of grasping to the impermanent, relative world. It is futile and causes suffering. As the poems indicate, both the Muslim Omar Khayam and the Christian William Blake also appreciated the illusory, shadowy and dreamlike nature of a reality that most humans generally take as solid and fixed, and suffer accordingly.

The universe is predictable and harmonious on very large scales. Einstein's Theory of General Relativity can predict with a very high degree of accuracy the movements of the stars, planets, solar systems and galaxies. Yet on the sub-atomic scale of quantum mechanics, nature seems fuzzy, indeterminate and subject to the laws of probability. So, scientifically speaking, whether our universe, our very existence, is marked by predictable harmony or cruel chance is largely a matter of perspective. The smaller scale can be understood by the probabilistic laws of quantum mechanics while the larger scale is quite predictable using the equations of Einstein's General Relativity. Up close, things appear disjointed, while the luxury of distance provides a more balanced view, like our analogy of the soldiers on the battlefield and the general far away.

A large part of our problem arises from taking any particular view as being *right* or *wrong*. Both General Relativity and the laws of Quantum Mechanics are required to get an understanding of how our universe works. At least until scientists come up with a unified theory to cover both large and small, we need them both.

If we can only appreciate the world conceptually, through the narrow aperture of intellect alone, then we limit ourselves to viewing life as composed only of individual beings and things, separate and fixed, some *right* and some *wrong*. If that's all we can appreciate, then we of course must align ourselves with what's *right* and condemn and fight against what's *wrong*. Endless conflict within ourselves and with others is the result.

But if we can also realize something larger, vaster and more all-encompassing, we can begin to generate a new reality for ourselves and our planet. This requires a lens opened wide, so wide that all normal facades disappear in the bright light of realization. As we have seen, this realization is expressed poetically not just by Buddha, but also by the Muslim and Christian traditions, as well as by others.

All these various traditions can speak of this realization because it is a capacity inherent in all of us, hidden only by an intellect that takes its own relative observations as being absolute. It does so out of a need to justify and bolster an ego-centered view that while not without its usefulness, can cause harm unknowingly. Because the ego, once born, finds itself a stranger in a strange land, and desperately seeks justification of its existence by identification with the products of its own construction: selfhood, inflexible views and a fixed reality.

The poems of Buddha, Omar Khayam and William Blake point to an understanding that quiets the anxiety of the ego's own noise, releasing it from this suffering and allowing for more mental spaciousness and peace. All three poems use the analogy of 'light' or the 'sun' as a central equivalence to the absolute view of Emptiness in Buddhism or Divinity in Middle Eastern and Christian traditions. In the poems attributed to Buddha and Omar Khayam, it is this 'light' and the light of the 'sun' which illumines and gives life to the world. Yet it is precisely because this 'light' is the absolute source of all life, each individual existence, whether a person or an animal, a rock or a cloud, an emotion or a thought, while a manifestation of that same light, is in itself a, "flash of lightning, a bubble in a stream, a phantom figure." All alike are impermanent and fleeting, yet powerful and significant.

William Blake teaches us why we fail to realize this and appreciate the world in this way. "We are led to believe a lie, when we see (with and) not thro' the eye." We generally view superficially only, looking "with" the eyes and categorizing and judging what we see only with a conditioned intellect. Blake advises us to see "thro' the eye", through the filters of perception we have inherited neurologically and which are further hardened and conditioned by culture. But seeing "thro' the eye" requires a deeper perceptual base than the superficial one we are inclined to rely on. Only then can we appreciate that, "what was born in a night, will perish in a night." Only then can we see that the relative world of perception is more fluid than fixed, more unknown than certain, more liberated than ensnared, more ungraspable than *real*. And existence is revealed as One by this *night* of unknowing. "While the soul slept…", I prefer the present tense, "…while the soul [sleeps], in beams of light." This deeper perceptual base does not categorize and judge for it 'sleeps' beyond the conditioning of time and culture, yet rejects not even these. This Mind is like an empty mirror which reflects all equally before it. It is merely the *light* that *shines*, as Maezumi Roshi said, "…totally impersonal and always at peace." Because the breath of this 'Soul' gives life to all, indeed *is* the life of *all*, it is not concerned with comings and goings, birth and death. This "Soul sleeps" in the midst of, and in the perfection of, the undivided activity of all its many forms.

We often take the various opposites of life's flow through time - God and man, good and evil, liberal and conservative, light and dark - as opposing armies that must fight for dominance. But the deeper perceptual base of which Buddha, Omar Khayam, and William Blake speak holds these phantoms as the very balancing mechanisms of its own existence.

Buddhism and Violence

There is a common misconception among many that all Buddhists are vegetarians and pacifists, and I suppose that's putting it kindly. Often we are viewed as just mushy-headed, tree-hugging new age space cadets. To some we are strange, and to others subversive. Even among my non-Buddhist friends of many years, I am considered somewhat odd. If they see me eating a hamburger they might say, "Aren't you a Buddhist? I thought all Buddhists were vegetarians." If I express a view that is not considered liberal, they might say, "But I thought you were a Buddhist. Aren't all Buddhists liberals?" Once, while playing golf, a close friend stood behind me and cast his shadow on my line of sight while I was putting (for money, no less!). When I politely asked him to move, he said, "Use your Buddhist concentration so it won't bother you." I immediately replied, "I'm using it to tell you to move out of the way!" He laughed and complied with my request. I sometimes think they'd be happy if I just doused myself with gasoline and lit myself on fire. Then perhaps they could happily nod at one another with the satisfaction of a stereotype fulfilled. "See! That's our friend. He's a *Buddhist*!"

The teaching of Emptiness is the core of Buddhist understanding. All things are empty of self-nature, impermanent and fleeting. But this is not a nihilistic view. Although the ocean is ungraspable, we thrive in the endless waves it produces. Indeed, we ourselves *are* those very waves and our True Nature is the ocean itself.

While this is true, although our *wisdom* can glimpse the eternal nature of its being, our *knowledge* is limited by the relative nature of all individual existence and perception. As I've tried to emphasize throughout this book, whatever we can see, hear, smell, taste, touch or understand is merely a temporary and fleeting manifestation of a larger matrix of existence, a larger movement of matter and energy of which we are but a small part.

All knowledge is empty. That doesn't mean it is not valuable. But it does mean, among other things, that it has natural limits. In his famous fascicle, *Genjokoan*, Master Dogen writes:

> "Since the place is here and the Way leads everywhere,
> The reason the limits of the knowable are unknowable is
> Simply that our knowledge arises with, and practices with,
> The absolute perfection of the Buddha-dharma."

In Zen, we and the Way are One. Although our experience as individuals is limited to here, the truth of the Way is found everywhere. In the actual dynamic vitality of this endless, revolving moment we call life, perceiver and perceived are one, there is no duality of subject and object. But knowledge is a snapshot of consciousness that seizes a moment and solidifies it into a conceptual file for storage and later use. It's like grabbing a cupful of water from a flowing river, and thinking that now you've grasped the whole stream. But as we can deduce from the history of all the sciences, our knowledge arises with, and changes with, the evolving flow of that very river.

Of course for a very long time, we had assumed that the objective world was separate from our subjective consciousness. It was there to be understood by us scientifically, and as knowledge progressed we could understand more and more, and use that knowledge, practice with it, as Dogen said, to our benefit. Of course this is true, and it is not my goal to disparage that pursuit.

But we now also know scientifically, in the study of Quantum Mechanics, that the answers we get from our observations are consistent with the questions we ask. We know that we cannot observe the quantum world without affecting it in some way. In this sense, it is impossible to separate ourselves from our observation. Subject and object are One in this dance of observation. We cannot look at the world on this level as if it were a separate objective and fixed reality we discover, then file away with perfect precision. We have finally seen and begun to understand that, on this level at least, our knowledge arises with the dance of observation of which we are an inextricable partner.

We practice with that very knowledge simply because complete precision of measurement is not possible. We must be open to the possibility and reality of the changing flowing stream which gives us life, which propels us forward, and which is ultimately the very flow of our lives and the flow of consciousness itself. And in this, even individual observation is but a momentary flash of brilliance at a particular point, in a particular direction, from a light that shines always and everywhere without limit. That flash of brilliance is our perception and our knowledge. That light is our True Nature, and realizing it is our wisdom.

Thus, any particular philosophy, whether it is one of dominance or one of peace, whether it preaches war or pacifism, is by nature limited by the knowledge that birthed it. The light that shines does not chose between any particular flash of its own brilliance. "The rain falls evenly on the just and the unjust."

When Two Swords Cross Points, There's No Need to Withdraw

Yet, as human beings, we must chose. Do we fight, or do we not? Is there a way consistent with enlightenment itself? Can we pick a path, a lifestyle, a philosophy, or a political party that espouses and follows a spiritually correct way? You might be able to. I cannot.

For in the end, I do not know. I do not believe that I can know. I started this chapter with a remembrance of my friend, Tom McGuinness, who was the co-pilot on American Flight 11 that was the first plane to hit the World Trade Center on September 11, 2001.

The man who sent terrorists to kill him, Osama bin Laden, is the world's current bogeyman. Hitler, Stalin, Khrushchev even Omar Khadaffi have faded into the background of our mythologies. Now we have someone new to focus on, to hate. It's easier than dealing with our own delusions and it seems more heroic.

It's interesting, but if there were no terrorist history surrounding Osama bin Laden and I were shown a picture of him, I would have assumed that he was a kind Islamic cleric. He has such a gentle face and always seems to be smiling. With all our abilities at photographic doctoring, I'm surprised we don't always see him with an evil grin. Maybe we could even take off the beard and paint in a thin Snidley Whiplash moustache.

In any case, I've wondered if I hate him. In truth, I do not. From the side of the Absolute, of course, Osama bin Laden is equally, "…a flash of lightning in a summer cloud, a phantom figure," like myself. But even from the Relative side of things, I don't consider myself better. Why? Because we are both products of the cause and effect of life's ceaseless flow. I suppose if I were in his shoes, i.e., had his genes, his parents, his schooling, his experiences and his money, I might do the same. I don't like to think in that way, but I am logically led to that conclusion.

But none of this means I wouldn't kill him. I have no hatred of the plants and animals I eat. Indeed, I have respect for them. I eat them anyway and I would hold no grudges should they eat me.

The great fear of fundamentalists and conservatives across the globe, I believe, is that if we let go of our mythologies of good and evil, we will be left defenseless in the face of those who still hold to them. Certainly, there is historical evidence to show that appeasement of an aggressive enemy has at times done nothing but encourage further aggression.

The great fear of many liberals is that if we become too aggressive, we will violate our values. Many Buddhist liberals feel that if they take a stand requiring violence, then they are somehow violating a basic principle of the enlightened life. And here it is also true that human delusion is a great causal factor in our blundering wars within ourselves and with each other.

The enlightened life is not something we can attain because it's not something we've ever lost. We can never violate it. This life *is* the enlightened life, no matter how it has evolved, and no matter what takes place. We only violate it in our own stories, by trying to separate ourselves from its functioning. Even the Dalai Lama has admitted that at times violence is justified. And again, once that position is maintained, what violence, when and to whom, becomes, regrettably, a political question. So there we are: back to a discussion, an argument, which never ends.

In politics, there often seems no end to the discord and disagreement. Propaganda, media control, suppression of the opposition, and outright extinction of the enemy have been the historical tools of politics. The arguments don't end; they just seem to get louder. Throughout history, churchmen, clerics and monks have genuflected, bowed, chanted and prayed for one side or the other, all the while thumping on some Bible, Koran or other dusty tome as divine justification for a glorification of one particular view over another.

Both of these extremes do little to help us maintain the delicate balance upon which life depends. Extreme views blind us and bind us just at the time when flexibility and appropriate responses are most called for.

Just as in the examples of air combat and Japanese swordfighting from the previous chapter, exaggerated maneuvers to win are born of the fixed views that are spawned by a fixed dualistic concept of self and other. In the political arena, these same extreme views produce arguments that never end because they are born and perpetuated by a conditioned perception of life that is merely expedient, not absolute. The history we have known is the history we are living, and the history we will create. It is the wheel of samsara and the reality of suffering we insist on perpetuating for ourselves and our planet. That is why the lesson that Buddha, Omar Khayam and William Blake teach us is so important to appreciate. In it, there is not only spiritual understanding, but there is hope.

All of Buddha's teaching is encapsulated in one word, one realization, *Shunyata* or *Emptiness*. This is the essential nature of all the myriad forms and places, including all the pairs of opposites. The co-arising of all the opposing forces is like a balancing mechanism that maintains the required homeostasis for life to exist. Without past or future, endlessly revolving, this Emptiness functions in one unceasing, yet timeless moment. Whether the turning of this dharma wheel is viewed as a grand success or a dismal failure is merely our own meager interpretation of its unfathomable brilliance.

It is said that Buddha is still practicing somewhere. Make that everywhere. All the manifestations of the essential wisdom of life seek true peace. It is merely a fact that it is no less difficult now than it has ever been. We naturally feel the strain of the balancing mechanisms of life's opposing arms that ceaselessly tug at our blood and brain, heart and sinews. We, indeed, are that very ebb and flow.

Buddha said that life is suffering. Our lives will inevitably meet the challenge of decay, death and resultant grief. This ceaseless change is an essential condition for life to exist. Yet we undoubtedly exacerbate the natural pain of this process by holding with a death grip to the neurologically inherited and culturally-conditioned delusions of the human mind.

Zen is important because its practice helps us to see through this veil and to realize our essential nature as nothing less than the empty and eternal light of the whole universe, which shines as the mists of both Buddha and Mohammed, terrorist and victim, you and me - transparent, ineffable and unmatched in splendor. This *mist* shines always and everywhere without limit in space or time. Many faces but only one mouth. Many dreams but only one dreamer.

CONCLUSION

Scientists tell us that the universe is approximately 13.7 billion years old and that our planet is close to 5 billion years old. The sun that gives us life and illumines our solar system is a 10 billion year star. So, by any outside estimate, the life of this planet is already halfway through its run.

Life, at least the nonmicrobial animal life we can easily recognize, only emerged around 500 million years ago. While our sun has another 5 billion years to burn, it will start heating up in around 200 million years, depending on whom you listen to. By around 500 million years from now, there will be no water on this planet as it will have all evaporated in the increasing heat. Of course, that means no more surfing.

So for a mere 1 billion years of time, only 10% of the possible lifetime of our planet, will there be anything that we generally point to as *life* existing here. As we know, Homo sapiens only emerged a few hundred thousand years ago. The consciousness that has emerged, and continues to emerge in our species, is what we perceive with, and deal with, today.

I find it remarkable that given the unbelievably tenuous nature of our existence, that we seem to find so much time and energy for creating misery. I recall listening to the late great basketball legend Pete Maravich talking about his interest in the game. When he learned about the history of our universe and the incredibly short span of human life on this planet, he said, "Hell. I'm playin' basketball!" I like his attitude.

Of course, we can't all play basketball, or surf all the time, or spend all our days dancing through fields of daffodils. Life can be a real test. There's no doubt about it. However, we can take some responsibility for our suffering. In Buddhism, our suffering arises in large part from our ignorance, our delusion. We can do something about that. As we've seen, Zen's practice and its realization are aimed at freeing us from these cells of our own making and releasing us into a new life, free from existential doubt, and with skillful means to deal with suffering more effectively.

I don't find the incredibly short span of human life on this planet to be a depressing fact. It actually makes life more poignant, more precious. In one sense, the relative sense, all our experience, life and death, and consciousness itself, is fleeting. In another sense, an absolute sense, all these waves of life and experience are in fact manifestations of something greater that is both ungraspable and unknowable. In Buddhism this is our True Nature. Although *unknowable*, it *can* be realized. In that realization there is refuge, there is peace.

And not just peace, but joy, as well. What a marvelous thing our lives are! What an unmatched miracle! All the great forces of the universe have met, merged, and evolved…into you. From morning to night in conscious light, and from night until morning in unconscious sleep, the forces of almost 14 billion years of time find their expression in your breath, your movement, your stillness, your laughter and your tears.

I don't know what conscious realms may exist elsewhere, or on some plane of existence after death...if any. It doesn't really matter. For like the depths of sleep, or meditation, unconscious states are the medicinal space where the activity of life is balanced. It is not really dead or vacant space, but a realm pregnant with possibility. And what we recognize consciously as activity, as life, is so permeated by the vast reaches of this emptiness, this still, permeable brilliance that births it, that the moment you think you've grasped the living essence of any moment, it disappears like a phantom in the dark. These two poles of life and death, light and dark, consciousness and unconsciousness, are perfectly merged in this moment and in you.

But look carefully. Did this moment ever start? How could it possibly ever end? We think we look into eternity when we gaze into space, but it's eternity that's gazing. And that's why Zen has great value. It can help us realize this important and liberating fact: that to have been born is indeed a blessing, and just to live...is enlightenment enough.